D0193614

About Richard Webster

Author of over thirty titles published with Llewellyn, Richard Webster is one of New Zealand's most prolific writers. His best-selling books include *Spirit Guides & Angel Guardians*, *Creative Visualization for Beginners*, *Soul Mates*, *Is Your Pet Psychic?*, *Practical Guide to Past-Life Memories*, *Astral Travel for Beginners*, *Miracles*, and the four-book series on archangels: *Michael*, *Gabriel*, *Raphael*, and *Uriel*.

A noted psychic, Richard is a member of the National Guild of Hypnotherapists (USA), the Association of Professional Hypnotherapists and Parapsychologists (UK), the International Registry of Professional Hypnotherapists (Canada), and the Psychotherapy and Hypnotherapy Institute of New Zealand. When not touring, he resides in New Zealand with his wife and family.

YOU CAN READ PALMS

RICHARD WEBSTER

Llewellyn Publications
Woodbury, Minnesota

First Edition
Second Printing, 2014

Cover design by Ellen Dahl
Interior art by Llewellyn art department; palm prints on pages 181 and 187 courtesy of the author

Llewellyn is a registered trademark of Llewellyn Worldwide, Ltd.

Library of Congress Cataloging-in-Publication Data
Webster, Richard, 1946–
    You can read palms / Richard Webster.—1st ed.
        p.   cm.
    Includes bibliographical references and index.
    ISBN 978-0-7387-1905-4
    1. Palmistry. I. Title.
    BF921.W435 2010
    133.6—dc22
                                    2009036594

Llewellyn Worldwide does not participate in, endorse, or have any authority or responsibility concerning private business transactions between our authors and the public.
    All mail addressed to the author is forwarded but the publisher cannot, unless specifically instructed by the author, give out an address or phone number.
    Any Internet references contained in this work are current at publication time, but the publisher cannot guarantee that a specific location will continue to be maintained. Please refer to the publisher's website for links to authors' websites and other sources.

Llewellyn Publications
A Division of Llewellyn Worldwide, Ltd.
2143 Wooddale Drive, Dept. 978-0-7387-1905-4
Woodbury, MN 55125-2989, U.S.A.
www.llewellyn.com

Printed in the United States of America

For my good friends,
Doug and Lynne Dyment

CONTENTS

List of Figures   xv

INTRODUCTION 1

1: FIRE, EARTH, AIR, AND WATER 9

Square-Shaped Palms   10
Oblong-Shaped Palms   10
Determining Finger Length   11
Putting It Together   13
The Four Elements   13
You and Your Friends   17
Other Methods of Classifying Hands   19
Hand Size   22

2: THE FINGERS 25

Phalanges   25
Finger Joints   26
Length of the Fingers   27

How the Hands Are Held 27
Finger Settings 28
Fingertips 29
Fingernails 30
Stress and Strain Lines 32
Mercury Finger (Little Finger) 32
Apollo Finger (Ring Finger) 34
Saturn Finger (Middle Finger) 36
Jupiter Finger (First Finger) 37
Leaning Fingers 39
Rings on the Fingers 41

3: THUMBS 43
Length of the Thumb 43
Willpower and Logic 44
Setting of the Thumb 46
Angle of the Thumb 46
Tip of the Thumb 48
Flexibility 49
The Wheat Line 50
Flower Line 50

4: THE MAIN LINES. 51
Heart Line 53
The Head Line 60
The Simian Crease 67
Life Line 69
Destiny Line 75

5: EXAMINING THE HAND. 83

Handshake   83
How the Hand Is Held   84
Consistency   84
Moist and Dry Hands   85
Skin Texture   85
Hair   86
Fingernails   86
Color   87
Flexibility   88

6: HOW TO GIVE A BRIEF PALM READING. . . . 89

7: THE MOUNTS. 97

The Mount of Venus   100
The Finger Mounts   102
The Mounts of Mars   106
The Plain of Mars   107
The Mount of Luna   108
The Mount of Neptune   109

8: THE MINOR LINES 111

The Health Line (Hepatica)   112
The Sun Line   113
The Line of Mars   115
Travel Lines   116
The Ring of Solomon   117
Line of Intuition   118

The Ring of Saturn   118
Via Lasciva   119
Loyalty Line   120
Mars Line   120
Relationship Lines   120
Children Lines   121
The Teacher's Square   122
Medical Stigmata   123
Indicators of Money   124
The Mystic Cross   125
The Rascettes   126

9: THE SKIN RIDGE PATTERNS. 129

Fingerprint Patterns   130
Tri-radii   136
Loop Patterns   139

10: OTHER MARKS ON THE PALM 147

Squares   147
Crosses   148
Triangles   149
Stars   150
Grilles   150
Circles   151
Dots and Spots   151
Islands   152
Chains   152

11: LOVE AND ROMANCE 155

Compatability   157
Hand Shapes   158
Heart Lines   158
The Thumb   160
Mount of Venus   160
Relationship Lines   161

12: CHOOSING A CAREER 163

Earth Hands (Square Palm, Short Fingers)   164
Air Hands (Square Palm, Long Fingers)   164
Fire Hands (Oblong Palm, Short Fingers)   165
Water Hands (Oblong Palm, Long Fingers)   165
Occupational Clues   166
Talents   168
Ambition   171

13: HOW TO TAKE HAND PRINTS 173

Taking a Print   174

14: PUTTING IT ALL TOGETHER 179

15: CONCLUSION 189

Notes   191
Glossary   193
Suggested Reading   201
Index   205

FIGURES

3A: First and Second Phalanges Equal in Length 45

4A: The Main Lines 52

4B: Mental Heart Line 54

4C: Physical Heart Line 55

4D: Heart Line Ending between Jupiter and
     Saturn Fingers 56

4E: Heart Line Ending under Jupiter Finger 57

4F: Heart Line Ending under Saturn Finger 58

4G: Heart Line with Islands 59

4H: Head Line Joined to Life Line at Start 61

4I: Head Line Starting Independently from Life Line . . 62

4J: Imaginative Head Line 63

4K: Practical Head Line 64

4L: Writer's Fork 65

4M: Simian Crease 68

4N: Life Line Hugging the Thumb 71

4O: Life Line Coming Well Across the Palm 71

4P: Sister Line 72

4Q: Worry Lines 72

4R: Destiny Line 76

7A: The Mounts................................. 98

8A: Hepatica................................... 113

9A: Whorl, Loop, and Arch—Fingerprint Patterns ... 131

9B: Tri-Radii................................... 137

9C: Loops in the Palm........................... 140

14A: Sample Print A 181

14B: Sample Print B 187

INTRODUCTION

PALMISTRY HAS BEEN AN INCREDIBLY useful skill for me. I was introduced to palmistry when I was ten years old. I had made friends with some neighbors, mainly because the wife was a good cook and I loved sampling her baking. Also, their house was the first I'd been in that had a large library, and I loved browsing through it. When I noticed all the books on palmistry on the shelves and started asking questions about them, the husband taught me the basics of the subject. He was a professional palmist, and I think it amused him to discuss the art with the kid from down the road.

I was a shy teenager, but I always found it easy to make friends because I could read palms. When I was twenty, I traveled around the world and made a comfortable living as a palmist in several different countries. I also made many lifelong friends through this work. Reading palms is a wonderful way to meet people wherever you happen to be, but more importantly, palmistry enables you to understand the motivations and needs of others, and it gives you the opportunity to help them.

Knowledge of palmistry is also useful in everyday life. There are many things you can tell about people from a glance at their hands. For instance, someone with short fingers is likely to prefer a quick, overall view of a situation, while someone with long fingers would want to know all the details. A person with long, oblong palms will be dreamy, and probably intuitive. However, someone with square-shaped palms will be more practical and down-to-earth. If I need to employ a builder or plumber, for instance, I will choose someone who has a good "Angle of Practicality" on his hands, as I know he will be good at the task. Knowledge of these things gives me an advantage in life.

Similarly, if I want to buy something and there are two checkout operators in the store, I would look to see which cashier has shorter fingers. I would line up in her line, as it will move faster than her colleague's line.

Obviously, if you can tell this much with a quick glance, you'll be able to tell much more from a detailed analysis of a person's hands. People's hands clearly reveal their character, and this tells you how they will react in any given situation. This, ultimately, reveals the sort of life they will experience. A high-strung, nervous introvert, for instance, is likely to lead a difficult life full of doubts, worries, and stress.

However, palmistry is not fatalistic. People can change if they want to. A good palmist can help people recognize their negative traits and provide suggestions for overcoming them.

I'm sure you'll enjoy exploring palmistry. The wonderful thing about palm reading is that you can start right away. There is no need to wait until you know all about the subject. Your friends and acquaintances will be only too pleased to show you their palms once they discover your new interest. Of course, you will not be able to tell them much at first. However, you'll quickly discover that no two hands are alike, and you'll be able to check for yourself everything that is included here.

At the end of the book, I've included a chapter on how to give proper readings. Once you reach this stage, you'll be well on the way to becoming a competent palm reader. I'm sure you'll find palmistry to be a useful skill that will enhance your life in many ways.

Palmistry is an ancient art that began during the Stone Age. Altamira, the innermost of the ancient Santander Caves in Spain, contains walls covered with paintings of human hands. The purpose of these paintings isn't known, but it certainly indicates the fascination Stone Age people had with hands.

Palm reading possibly began in India or China thousands of years ago. Cheiro,[1] a famous palmist who lived during the early twentieth century, claimed to have seen one of the ancient Indian Vedic scriptures containing information about palmistry.

Katharine St. Hill, author of *The Book of the Hand*, wrote, "The oldest manuscript that the world knows of, found among the venerable papyri of Egypt, is a prescription for the composition of women's face-paint, or 'make-up,' and the second is a treatise on hand-readings."[2]

Some 2,500 years ago, Aristotle briefly mentioned palmistry in his books *Historia Animalium* and *Problemata* 10 and 34. There is an old story that says Aristotle became interested in the subject after finding an ancient Arabic book on palmistry sitting on an altar dedicated to Hermes. Because of this, Alexander the Great, who was extremely interested in divination, asked Aristotle to write a book on palmistry for him. Unfortunately, although it's a charming story, there is no evidence whatsoever to support it.

Palmistry was also practiced in ancient Rome, and Pliny and Juvenal both mentioned the subject in their works. In his autobiography, the Emperor Hadrian mentioned that when he was a child, his grandfather predicted a great future for him after reading his palms.

Avicenna, an eleventh-century Arab physician, wrote about the meanings of different hand shapes in his *Canon of Medicine*. His book was largely responsible for an upsurge of interest in palmistry during the twelfth and thirteenth centuries.

In his book, *Policraticus*, John of Salisbury (c. 1115–1180) mentioned palmistry as a new type of divination, which indicates that palmistry did not become popular in the West until the middle of the twelfth century.

Gypsies have always been associated with palmistry. As they crossed Europe, Sigismund, the Holy Roman Emperor, used them as spies. This did not remain a secret for long, and when they reached the gates of Paris in 1427, they were not allowed into the city. However, the worthy citizens of Paris, intrigued and captivated by the exotic strangers, rushed outside to have their palms read as soon as the gates opened the next morning.

The ancient tradition of crossing a gypsy's palm with silver dates from this time. The church warned people to keep away from gypsies, who were labeled servants of the devil. To counter this, the gypsies explained that the devil was afraid of both silver and the sign of the cross. If you made a sign of the cross over a gypsy's hand with silver, you were protected. Naturally, the gypsy kept the silver as part of a fee.

The invention of the printing press dramatically increased the number of books on palmistry, which enabled many more people to learn about the subject. One of the first of these books—*Die Kunst Chiromantia* by Johannes Hartlieb (c. 1410–1468), a Bavarian physician—was published in 1448.

Unfortunately, though, most of these books perpetuated superstitious, outdated ideas. It wasn't until the nineteenth century that two remarkable Frenchmen transformed palmistry by looking at the subject in a more scientific manner.

The first of these was a retired army officer named Captain Casimir Stanislaus D'Arpentigny (1798–1865). His interest in palmistry began when he was a young man, after a gypsy girl read his palms. He started searching for old palmistry texts and ultimately began looking at people's hands. When he retired from the army, he became friendly with a wealthy landowner who was interested in science whose wife was just as interested in the arts. Both of them held regular parties for their friends, and D'Arpentigny, who was interested in both the arts and science, was a regular guest. He was fascinated to discover that the landowner's friends had fingers containing knotted joints, while the wife's artistic friends all had smooth fingers. D'Arpentigny began studying palmistry seriously and published his book *La Chirognomie* in 1843. D'Arpentigny had no interest whatsoever in the lines of the hand. He focused entirely on the shape and texture of the hand and the length of the fingers. As a result of his studies, he became the first person to classify hands by their shapes. Even today, some palmists still use the classification system he developed.

Adrien Adolphe Desbarolles (1801–1886), a portrait painter, was the next person to influence palmistry. He had been studying the Cabala with Eliphas Lévi, a famous French occultist. One day, the subject of palmistry came up, and Lévi suggested to Desbarolles that he study palmistry to see if he could bring it up to date. After reading everything he could find on the subject, Desbarolles began reading palms professionally, and he ultimately wrote two monumental books on the subject. Unlike D'Arpentigny, Desbarolles's main interest was the lines on the palm.

The next major contribution to palmistry occurred in the United States when William G. Benham published *The Laws of Scientific Hand Reading* in 1900. He had studied the works of D'Arpentigny and Desbarolles and believed an accurate interpretation could be made only after studying both the shape and the lines of the hand. Benham believed that palms could be read scientifically, and no psychic ability was necessary.

In 1944, *The Hands of Children* by Julius Spier (1887–1942) was published. It contained an introduction by Carl Jung and was the first major book that used palmistry for psychological analysis. This book was intended to be the first of a trilogy, but sadly, the author died two years before it was published.

Since 1965, the dedicated staff at the Kennedy-Galton Centre in Harrow, North London, have been studying skin ridge patterns to ascertain whether the hands can determine health factors. More than four thousand scientific papers have been written on this subject, demonstrating how important this area of research is to medicine.

Dermatoglyphics, the study of the skin ridge patterns, is now taught to medical students at many German universities. Computer programs have also been developed in Germany to enable rapid assessment of people's hands. These analyses can predict with eighty percent accuracy the chances of a newborn baby developing a variety of illnesses, including cancer, heart disease, diabetes, and mental illness.

Nothing could be more important than health, and the future of palmistry is assured now that scientists are studying skin ridge patterns and rediscovering information that palmists have always known. Since the 1970s, many books have been written on the medical applications of dermatoglyphics.[3]

Palmistry has survived since Stone Age times and is no longer simply a method of divination. I believe the most exciting chapters in the history of palmistry are yet to be written.

1

...

FIRE, EARTH, AIR, AND WATER

WE'LL START EXPLORING PALMISTRY BY classifying people into different groups determined by the shapes of their hands. This branch of palmistry is known as *cheirognomy*. Many people think that palmistry is concerned solely with the lines on the palm of the hand, but this is only part of the subject. Classifying hand shapes is a useful skill.

Start by looking at your own palms. Mentally remove your fingers and thumbs, and see if your palms are square or oblong in shape. This is the first thing to look at when looking at peoples' hands. Making this first observation divides all of humanity into two groups: those with square palms and those with oblong. However, you are going to gradually add to this, so that, with practice, you'll be able to instantly classify someone's hand and determine a great deal from it.

Square-Shaped Palms

Square-shaped palms are usually wide. The larger this square shape is, the more stamina and energy the person will possess. People with square-shaped palms are practical, capable, down-to-earth people with a positive approach to life. They are good workers and have enough stamina and energy to work for long periods of time when necessary. They enjoy being busy.

Oblong-Shaped Palms

Palms that are longer in length than breadth are considered oblong palms. People with palms like these are imaginative, dreamy, intuitive, and frequently creative. They are full of ideas, but they sometimes find it hard to get motivated into action. They need plenty of variety in their lives, as they get bored easily. The longer the palm is in comparison to the breadth, the more pronounced these qualities are. Artists like to draw hands that are long and graceful. These hands might look beautiful, but are not necessarily useful in everyday life.

Occasionally, you'll come across a palm that is broad, but also slightly oblong. People with palms like these are practical dreamers. If you look at someone's palm and find it hard to decide whether it is square or oblong, you will have found a practical dreamer.

You'll discover that most of your friends will have palm shapes that are similar to your own. This is not surprising, as like-minded people tend to become friends. In fact, with a bit of practice, you could determine which people in a crowded room are most likely to be friends. Of course, this does not work all the time, as opposites frequently attract as well.

Once you are able to determine the shapes of people's palms, you can start looking at the fingers. Fingers are considered to be either short or long. This is easy to figure out when the fingers are obviously one length or the other. Unfortunately, a lot of people cannot be classified that easily, as they have medium-length fingers. Let's look at all three possibilities.

Determining Finger Length

The standard way to determine finger length is to ask people to fold their fingers over their palms and notice how far down the palms they can reach. If they reach a spot at least seven-eighths of the way down the palm, the fingers are considered to be long. However, it is not quite that easy, as some people are more flexible than others, which means they can reach farther down their palms than someone with more rigid hands.

Determining finger length might be difficult at first. However, with practice, you will be able to determine the length of someone's fingers at a glance.

SHORT FINGERS

People with short fingers become impatient with details. They need to be busy and are frequently involved in several different things at the same time. They are often better at starting projects than they are at finishing them. Short-fingered people are interested in a wide variety of activities, and are likely to know a little bit about many different things, rather than a great deal about any one subject.

LONG FINGERS

People with long fingers are good with details. They enjoy exploring subjects in depth. Anything they become involved in needs to have a great deal to it. If it is too simple, they lose interest. They are patient and enjoy solving problems.

MEDIUM-LENGTH FINGERS

Not surprisingly, people with medium-length fingers are a mixture of the other two types. They are reasonably patient and can be good with details when they have to be. However, they can also be impulsive at times and skim over the surface of things, rather than exploring topics in greater depth.

Putting It Together

You can now combine this knowledge to create four possibilities: square palms with short fingers, square palms with long fingers, oblong palms with short fingers, and oblong palms with long fingers.

The Four Elements

Thousands of years ago, a concept known as the four elements evolved. These four elements of fire, earth, air, and water were considered the building blocks of life, and people believed that everything in the universe was created from them. Of course, people no longer believe this, but the system has remained because it provides a convenient and effective method of classification. For example, the twelve signs of the zodiac all belong to different elements. Aries, Leo, and Sagittarius belong to the fire element. Taurus, Virgo, and Capicorn belong to the earth element. Gemini, Libra, and Aquarius belong to the air element. Cancer, Scorpio, and Pisces belong to the water element.

If you belong to one of the fire signs, you are likely to be enthusiastic, excitable, and adventurous. If your sign is one of the earth signs, you are likely to be reliable, determined, and patient. If your sign belongs to the air element, you will enjoy communication and new ideas. If your sign is a water sign, you will be imaginative, intuitive, and sensitive.

Not surprisingly, the four hand-shape combinations also correspond neatly with the four elements. However, the chances are that your hand shape will not belong to the same element as your horoscope sign. This is because your horoscope sign is just a small part of your total makeup. Your horoscope sign is determined by the position of the sun at your time of birth, but in order to construct a complete horoscope chart, the positions of every planet need to be taken into consideration. Consequently, you might be a Taurus (earth sign) but have four planets in Leo (fire sign). This means that you are likely to display more of the characteristics of fire than you would of earth, even though your sun sign, or horoscope sign, happens to be of earth.

FIRE HANDS

Keywords: Inspirational, enthusiastic, exciting, action.

A fire hand consists of an oblong palm and short fingers. The fingers are always shorter than the palm. Fire is an interesting element as it heats and warms, but can also burn. Consequently, people with this type of hand overreact at times. People with this sort of hand are enthusiastic, creative, and constantly busy. They are fun to be around. The short fingers provide spontaneity and a dislike of detail, while the oblong palm provides intuition. These people are usually extroverts who need to be busy to be happy. However, they do not like being told what to do and prefer occupations that provide scope for them to use their own initiative. They find it hard to sit still and recreational activities are likely to involve physical activity, such as a sport, or challenge them in some way. People with fire hands are natural risk-takers.

People with fire hands get on well with people who have air hands. However, they are likely to have problems with people who have water hands. Water puts out fire, and people with water hands can quench a fire-handed person's natural enthusiasm. This also reveals another aspect of the fire hand. Although people with water hands are emotional, the fire person is likely to keep his or her emotions in check and respond to any difficulty with action.

EARTH HANDS

Keywords: Practical, reliable, dependable, strong.

The earth hand contains a square palm with short fingers. The palm is usually hard, and the fingers are stiff. People with these hands are practical, stable, reliable, down-to-earth, and easy to get along with. However, just like the earth itself, these people can occasionally erupt and react violently. These people enjoy routine, repetitive physical work, and they are usually good with their hands. They work steadily and consistently, and they hate being rushed. They are possessive, stubborn, honest, loyal, and cautious. They constantly seek security. They enjoy being outdoors and often prefer to live in the country, rather than endure the hustle and bustle of a city. They are not interested in change or innovation unless they can put it to practical use. Most of the time they are happy with methods that have stood the test of time.

In the past, people with earth hands worked mainly in agriculture, but today they can be found in any down-to-earth, practical field. They enjoy occupations that are practical and make use of their hands. They make wonderful employees who are often overlooked as they arrive on time and immediately start work. They are hard working, reliable, and loyal.

People with earth hands get on best with people who also have earth hands. They also get on well with people who have water hands.

AIR HANDS

Keywords: Intellectual, communicative, logical.

People with air hands have square palms and long fingers. Their palms usually contain many lines. These people are practical thinkers who use logic more than their intuition. They like mental challenges and enjoy learning. They also enjoy communicating with others, and many make a career from some form of communication—teaching, writing, and acting are good examples. Air-handed people are quick thinkers who express themselves clearly. They are emotionally well adjusted and seldom get upset. Most people with air hands live in a world of thoughts and they pay little attention to their hearts.

People with air hands get on well with people who have fire hands.

WATER HANDS

Keywords: Sensitive, emotional, imaginative, intuitive.

People with water hands have oblong palms and long fingers. These are the hands that artists love to draw, because they are long and graceful. People with water hands are sensitive, changeable, emotional, easily hurt, and highly intuitive. In fact, this hand is sometimes known as the intuitive hand. People with this type of hand are gentle, refined, and have good taste. They also have a rich inner life, as their imagination is vivid, and they create elaborate fantasies in their minds. They are drawn to the mystical and spiritual aspects of life. People with water hands are happiest when they are in love. The biggest problem people with water hands have is a reluctance to act on their feelings.

People with water hands possess a natural empathy with others. Consequently, they often work in humanitarian fields, such as healing or counseling. It is important that any work they do involves their feelings in some way.

People with water hands get on well with people with earth hands.

You and Your Friends

Look at the hands of your friends and determine what shapes their hands are. See how well they fit the previous descriptions. You may not have friends who represent all four elements, but try to find someone to represent each basic type. This makes it much easier to remember the basic characteristics of each type. If, for instance, you know that your friend Derek has an air hand, all you need do is think of him and his personality, and the characteristics of the air hand will immediately come into your mind.

I know people from all four groups, but my friends belong to air, fire, and water. I use a former client of mine if I want an example of an earth person.

Jason is a good example of an earth person. He is a professional jockey who adores horses and gardening. He enjoys the excitement of racing but is happiest at home, working in his garden. He has an incredible empathy for animals, and has several pets that he has rescued from animal shelters. He has recently taken up woodcarving as a hobby.

Barbara has an air hand. She edits a women's magazine and enjoys all the activity and business associated with weekly deadlines. She is constantly planning several issues ahead, while at the same time looking after a family of teenagers.

Ken has a fire hand. He's a theatrical producer who has made and lost several fortunes over the years. He now has a business partner who looks after the financial aspects of his various activities. Hopefully, this time he'll be able to keep some of the money he earns. Ken is the most excitable person I've ever met. He's overflowing with enthusiasm for his latest stage show, and is totally convinced it will be a success. I love spending time with him but sometimes it's a relief to leave him too, as his exuberant enthusiasm for everything that catches his attention can get wearing after a while.

Laura has a water hand. She is a successful writer of romance novels, yet constantly worries about money and her family. She also worries about her career and wonders if she might not be better suited to working in the fashion industry or interior design. She works best in bursts: she'll spend months thinking about her next book, and then write it in a week.

I find it fascinating that all of these people, my friends, are all so true to their hand shapes. Obviously, there is much more to their characters than what is prescribed by their hand shapes, and all of that is revealed in other aspects of their hands. You will find it an easy way to learn the four basic types by finding people of each type to act as your mental picture for each one.

Other Methods of Classifying Hands

Casimir D'Arpentigny was the first person to classify people by their hand shapes. Today palmists take this method of categorizing people for granted, and we tend to forget what an incredible contribution D'Arpentigny made to the art of palmistry. Unfortunately, his classification system has become outdated. It was useful in his day, when most people lived in the country and worked in the fields, but it is difficult to classify people using his system today. However, many palmists still use it, and I include it here for the sake of completeness.

I was taught D'Artepigny's system when I was a boy. Even though I use the four-element system most of the time, every now and again I'll classify a hand using the seven shapes that Casimir D'Arpentigny devised: elementary, spatulate, conic, square, knotty, pointed, and mixed. The shapes you're likely to see most often are the conic and knotty hands.

ELEMENTARY HANDS

The elementary hand has a square palm and short, stubby fingers. The skin is coarse, and there are few lines on the palm. People with elementary hands are good workers, but they are inclined to stubbornness and violence when their needs are not being met.

SPATULATE HANDS

The spatulate hand comes in two forms: either the palm is narrower at the base or the fingertips, or the hand has fingers that widen at the tips, making them look like a spatula. People with spatulate hands are practical, energetic, impulsive, creative, and confident of their abilities.

CONIC HANDS

Conic hands are graceful and attractive. They taper slightly at the base of the palm and at the fingers. The fingers are medium to long and have rounded tips. People with conic hands have good taste and work best in attractive surroundings. They are usually followers rather than leaders.

SQUARE HANDS

Square hands have a square palm and medium-length fingers with square tips. People with square hands are capable, orderly, and methodical. They dislike change and uncertainty.

KNOTTY HANDS

I've never liked the term "knotty hands." D'Arpentigny described them as philosophic hands, and this is what I prefer to call them. Philosophic hands have pronounced finger joints. People with philosophic hands like to analyze and think matters through before acting. If the knots are on the joints closest to the fingertips, the person is likely to enjoy arguments and intense discussions.

POINTED HANDS

Again, this is a term I've never liked. D'Arpentigny described these hands as psychic, and this is what I prefer to call them. Psychic hands are long and thin, and the fingers have pointed tips. People with psychic hands are idealistic dreamers who are easily influenced by the ideas and opinions of others.

MIXED HANDS

D'Arpentigny used the term "mixed hands" to describe people who had hands that did not fit into any of the other categories. Unfortunately, that describes most people, and this is the major stumbling block to D'Arpentigny's system.

There are a number of other classification systems that you will come across. In the nineteenth century, Carl Carus (1789–1869), physician to the king of Saxony, devised a system of four shapes that he called elementary, motoric, sensitive, and psychic. Traditional Chinese palmistry uses five shapes: earth, wood, fire, water, and metal. William Benham named the seven types in his system after the planets, creating Jupiterian, Saturnian, Apollonian, Mercurian, Martian, Lunarian, and Venusian.

You might want to investigate some of the other classifications later. As it is better to master one system before looking at anything else, practice with the four elements until you have it mastered, and then, possibly look at some of the others.

Hand Size

Once you start looking at hands, you will notice that some people have large hands in comparison to the rest of their body, while others have smaller hands. You need to evaluate this carefully, as a short person is likely to have smaller hands than someone who is tall.

You would expect people with large hands to work with large objects. However, the opposite is usually the case. People with large hands enjoy working with small things, or in an enclosed space. Jewelers and dentists, for instance, are likely to have large hands. People who deal with figures also often have large hands. These people are generally neat and tidy, and store items in specific places so that they can easily find them again.

People with small hands like to work on large-scale undertakings. They have big ideas and plans, and are usually better at the overall picture, rather than the fiddly details. I once knew someone who produced a new magazine. Unfortunately, the venture failed as he had totally forgotten about arranging distribution for the finished publication. He had small hands.

You can now divide people into four groups, determined by their hand shapes. Obviously, people are much more complex than this, but this elemental system creates a good basis to work from. It is rare to find someone who is totally fire, earth, air, or water. Occasionally, you'll find a hand that is hard to fit into any of the elements, but with practice you'll find that most hands are relatively easy to place into one of the four categories.

In the next two chapters, you'll learn how to examine the fingers and thumbs to provide additional information to modify and enhance what you have learned from the shape of the hands.

2

...

THE FINGERS

You ALREADY KNOW THAT FINGERS can be short, medium, or long. No matter what length they are, they should be straight. Fingers that curve toward other fingers are gaining support from them. This means that the person is subconsciously holding himself or herself back.

Phalanges

Each finger is divided into three sections, known as phalanges. We can tell a great deal about someone from the size and shape of each of these sections. Ideally, each phalange should be approximately the same size as the other phalanges on the same finger. If one phalange is longer than the other phalanges on the same finger, the person will be using the energies of that phalange at the expense of the others. For instance, it is very common for the tip phalange of the little finger to be longer than the other two.

The *tip phalange* relates to intuition and spirituality. If someone has a long tip phalange on each finger, he or she will be thoughtful and caring, and will ultimately develop a strong faith.

The *middle phalange* relates to the intellect. Someone who has long middle phalanges will have a good brain, and he or she will use it well in everyday life.

The *base phalange*, nearest the palm, relates to the material aspects of life. Someone with long base phalanges needs comfort and some of the luxuries of life to feel completely happy.

If a person's base phalanges are thick compared to the other phalanges, he or she will enjoy comfort and luxury. If these phalanges are both thick and spongy, the person will appreciate good food and is likely to be a good cook.

Finger Joints

There are two possibilities here. If a person's joints, or knots, are almost invisible, he or she is said to have smooth joints. If the joints are very visible, the person is said to have knotty fingers. With most people, the joints nearest the fingers are more noticeable than the ones nearer the fingertips.

Joints give a clue as to how the person thinks. Someone with knotty fingers likes to analyze things and work them out carefully before acting. Knotty-fingered people will enjoy lengthy discussions, and may even provoke arguments for the sheer joy of expressing their points of view. I like to imagine thoughts coming in through the fingertips, and going round and around in circles whenever they reach a knot, before carrying on to the palm itself.

Someone with smooth fingers relies more on inspiration and will have no desire to analyze everything the way the knotty-fingered person does. Smooth-fingered people will be spontaneous and intuitive. There are many more smooth-fingered people in the world than there are knotty-fingered people.

Length of the Fingers

Fingers vary in length. With most people, the middle finger is the longest. However, I have met a few people with middle fingers that are shorter than the fingers on either side. When you start looking at people's hands, you will notice the many possible variations in finger length. All of these variations can be interpreted, and they will be discussed later in this chapter, in the sections that cover the fingers individually.

How the Hands Are Held

When someone shows his or her palms to you, the fingers will be held either close together, or separated from each other. If the fingers are held together, it means that the person is cautious, and possibly worried about what you might see in his or her palms. It also means that he or she can keep a secret. If the fingers are held wide apart, it is a sign that the person is open and confident. This person probably enjoys shocking others with words. It's a sign of an independent thinker when the fingers are held slightly apart.

Interestingly, people who hold their hands with the fingers together are better at hanging on to money than people who have the fingers held apart. They let money "slip through their fingers."

It can be useful to collect tracings of people's hands to look at while you are learning. Ask the person whose hands you are going to trace to shake their hands for a few seconds to make them free and loose. Then ask them to place them, palms downward, on a sheet of paper. Using a pen or pencil, make a tracing of the person's hands. Make sure that you write the person's name on each tracing and also record if they are right- or left-handed. Having a collection of tracings means that you can check everything you learn about hand and finger shapes on the hands of your friends. This will also help you understand why your friends act in the particular ways they do.

Finger Settings

The fingers can be mounted on the palms in four different ways. If the base of the fingers creates a gentle curved arch, the person will be responsible, well-balanced, sympathetic, and able to stand up for him- or herself.

If both the index and little fingers are set lower than the middle fingers, the person will lack confidence in his or her own abilities. This person will be diffident and hesitant in most social situations.

If the fingers are set in a straight line the person will be full of confidence, and will enjoy showing off abilities to others.

If the fingers are set in a slight curve, but the little finger is set noticeably lower than the others, the person will experience a number of setbacks as he or she progresses through life. He or she will learn from each setback, but most of the time the lessons are learned the hard way. A low-set little finger used to be rare, but is common nowadays. This is possibly due to the fast pace of life today. A low-set little finger is known as a "dropped" little finger.

Fingertips

Fingertips can be classified into four types: conic, pointed, square and spatulate. The most commonly found type is called conic. These are gently rounded tips to the fingers. People with tips of this sort are easygoing, practical, and quick thinkers.

If the fingertips are almost pointed, the person will be idealistic, sensitive, intuitive and highly strung. Someone with pointed fingertips on every finger will have a dreamy, unrealistic approach to life.

When the fingertips appear to be square in shape, the person will be methodical, practical, and pragmatic. Enjoying system and order, this person will be cautious when it comes to trying something new or different.

The fourth type is almost the opposite of the square-tipped person. This type is known as spatulate. Spatulate fingers appear to flare out slightly at the ends. People with these are restless, inventive, unconventional, and always busy.

Fingernails

Even the fingernails can be interpreted. Average-length fingernails are approximately half as long as the tip phalange of the finger they are on. If the nails are longer than this, the person lives in his or her imagination most of the time. If the nails are short, compared to the length of the tip phalange, the person will be rigid, critical, and distrustful of others.

If the fingernails are narrow, the person will be narrowminded and possessive. It is extremely difficult to persuade those with narrow nails to change their minds once a decision has been made. Someone with wide fingernails will be broadminded, active, and easy to get along with.

As the fingernails grow quickly, they reveal what has been occurring in the person's body over the previous six months. Consequently, they can reveal the state of the person's health.

Nail color is an important health indicator. Most people are surprised to learn that their fingernails are actually clear. The color is determined by the flesh beneath the nails.

Normal nails are pinkish in color. This pink is similar to, but slightly stronger than, the flesh of the fingers. Deep red nails are a sign of possible high blood pressure.

White nails are a sign of anemia. Someone with white nails will feel lethargic and tired most of the time. He or she will also feel the cold more than others.

Light blue nails are usually a sign that the person is recovering from an illness, and his or her immune system has not fully healed. Dark blue nails indicate poor circulation.

Purple nails can indicate high blood pressure and hardening of the arteries.

It can be a sign of jaundice if the nails appear yellow, especially on the edges. This can also be a sign of liver and kidney problems.

White spots on the nails reveal nervousness, anxiety, and stress. A number of small spots indicates a variety of stresses in the person's life. He or she is rundown and needs a vacation.

Horizontal ridges across the nail indicate a temporary health concern, such as an accident, illness, operation, or sudden shock.

Vertical ridges can indicate bronchial problems, such as colds, bronchitis, allergies, and asthma.

The moons are the small white semi-circles at the base of the fingernails. They reveal information about the heart and circulation of blood. It is unusual to see a thumb without moons, but you find many people with no moons on their fingernails. If no moons are shown on the fingernails, the person's circulation is not working as well as it should.

Large moons indicate low blood pressure. People with large moons are active and vital, and enjoy all the good things life has to offer.

Now we're going to look at the individual fingers and see what we can learn from them.

Stress and Strain Lines

Horizontal lines on the tip sections of the fingers are known as stress lines. They show that the person has been in a stressful situation for a long time. They take time to appear, and also disappear slowly once the stressful situation has been resolved.

Strain lines are much less important, and they appear and disappear quickly. Strain lines are fine vertical lines on the section of the fingers closest to the palm. These lines appear when the person needs a day or two of rest. He or she may have been overworking, is due for a vacation, or is going to bed too late every night.

Mercury Finger (Little Finger)

We'll start with the little finger. In palmistry, it is known as the Mercury finger. In Roman times, Mercury was the winged messenger of the gods. Consequently, the little finger is the finger of communication, in all its various forms.

An average-length little finger reaches up to about the first joint of the ring (third) finger. This shows that the person is reasonably good at some form of communication. If it is longer, the communication abilities are increased. Someone with a long little finger will be good at self-expression and can be extremely persuasive. This person will be a good talker and a natural salesperson.

The opposite situation occurs when the little finger is noticeably short. This person will have problems in expressing his or her thoughts. This combination can also make the person impulsive and willing to take risks that other people would hesitate to attempt.

Many people have a little finger that is set low on the palm. This can sometimes make an average length Mercury finger appear short. If you look at where the fingers join the palm, you will notice that they usually create a slight curve or form a reasonably straight line at the edge of the palm. If the little finger is set noticeably below the place where the other fingers join the palm, it is called a "dropped" little finger. These people often have to learn the hard way and make many mistakes as they go through life. If the little finger is dropped, you will have to mentally raise it to the level of the other fingers to determine if the finger is short, average, or long. A dropped little finger is usually a sign of shyness, even though the person might try to conceal that trait.

The tip phalange of this finger is usually the longest. This is the area of verbal communication. Most people express themselves best by talking, so it is not surprising that this phalange is emphasized on most people. A good length tip phalange is essential for anyone who makes a living using his or her voice. Entertainers, teachers, radio and television personalities, auctioneers, and salespeople are all examples of people who use their voice along with other skills to make a living.

The middle phalange governs written communication. This is the smallest phalange for most people, as they find it hard to express themselves with words on paper. When this phalange is large, you will have found someone who can write a good letter or report. Naturally, most authors have a large second phalange on their little fingers.

The base phalange relates to the material world. If this phalange is the largest, the person will be interested in making money, and will use his or her communication skills to get ahead.

Apollo Finger (Ring Finger)

The ring finger is named after Apollo, the Greek and Roman god of music and poetry. Consequently, it's not surprising that this finger represents creativity and beauty. An average Apollo finger reaches halfway up the fingernail of the second finger, and is about the same length as the first finger.

The three phalanges, or sections, on this finger are usually equal in length. People with equal length phalanges on this finger enjoy surrounding themselves with attractive things, and work best in pleasant surroundings.

If the tip phalange is longer than the others, it is a sign that the person has a good imagination, and is usually creative. There are other areas of the hand that need to be looked at to confirm this, and we'll cover them later. Even if not creative in an artistic sense, this person will be a highly creative thinker. This person will be restless and look at life in a holistic, forward-looking manner.

If the second phalange is longer than the others, the person will possess good taste, and would work best in a career that used this talent. These people enjoy discussing and thinking about artistic and creative activities. Likely to be intelligent, this person will have a keen sense of the ridiculous.

It is unusual for the base phalange to be the longest. The base phalanges all relate to physicality. Consequently, when someone with a long base phalange on this finger expresses him- or herself creatively, it is likely to be something physical, such as dancing or sport. However if nothing else in the person's hand relates to creativity, a long base phalange means that the person has no real feel for beauty but tries to impress others with possessions.

In palmistry, we are always looking for balance. Ideally, the Apollo finger and Jupiter (first) finger should be approximately equal in length. Most people have an Apollo finger that is slightly longer than the Jupiter finger and this is considered average. If the Apollo finger is considerably longer than the Jupiter finger, the person will appear to be a confident, outward-looking individual, but will have private doubts about self-worth.

If the Apollo finger is long, but the Jupiter finger is short, the person will be inclined to show off and take unnecessary risks.

If the Apollo finger is short, the person will have little interest in the arts, and this lack of interest is often revealed in his or her choice of clothing and décor. Much of the positivity provided by the Apollo finger is lost when this finger is short, and this creates a slightly negative approach to life, especially when problems occur.

Saturn Finger (Middle Finger)

The middle finger is named after Saturn, the Roman god of time. He had a gloomy, austere, introspective nature, which explains why his name was given to this finger. The Saturn finger relates to duty, responsibility, common sense, restrictions, and limitations. Because of this, the Saturn finger also relates to the community the person lives in.

The Saturn finger should be the longest finger on the hand. If it is not, it shows that the person lacks responsibility, and will find it hard to work as part of a group. He or she will have a strong, private, and intense inner life that is seldom, if ever, shared with others.

The Saturn finger is considered long if at least half of its tip phalange is above the other fingers. Someone with this formation will find it hard to relax in the company of others and will be a loner or a misfit. Despite having difficulties in gaining the support of others, this individual will have strong ideas about the community as a whole, and will work hard to make them real. This person will also have a strong sense of tradition.

If the Saturn finger is short, but still reaches beyond the Apollo and Jupiter fingers, the person will suffer from stress and frustration caused by difficulty in conforming to the rules of society.

A tip phalange of this finger that is longer than the others indicates intelligence and the tendency to look down on others. This person will possess strong inner beliefs relating to a sense of duty and responsibility to the various groups or organizations he or she may belong to.

Someone with the second phalange longer than the others will enjoy doing skilled, technical work. If the finger also has smooth joints, an interest in psychic matters is likely. This person will also enjoy sharing insights on the local community, country, world, and even universe, with others.

Traditional interpretation says that when the base phalange is the longest, the person will be interested in agriculture. Gardeners, and other people who enjoy working with the land, usually have long base phalanges on this finger. However, this phalange also shows the person is reliable, loyal, dependable, and honest. If such a person makes a promise, you can be certain that it will be kept. This person will expect total honesty from friends too, and will be bitterly disappointed when let down by others.

Jupiter Finger (First Finger)

The index, or first, finger is named after Jupiter, the supreme god in Roman mythology. Not surprisingly, this finger is related to enthusiasm, energy, ambition, the ability to lead, and the ego. It is the finger of self-esteem.

In palmistry, we are always looking for balance. Consequently, the Jupiter finger should reach between half and two-thirds of the way up the tip phalange of the Saturn finger. It should be approximately the same length as the Apollo finger.

If this finger is longer than the Apollo finger, the person will possess drive and ambition. Someone with long Jupiter fingers has a strong inner need to be successful, and is prepared to work long and hard to achieve it.

If the Jupiter finger is almost as long as the Saturn finger, the person will be ambitious and have a drive to achieve set goals. This person will also be sociable, generous, and possess a big appetite for all life has to offer. He or she will also possess a strong ego.

If this finger is about the same length as the Apollo finger, the person will be moderately ambitious, but will be more realistic about chances of success than someone with a longer Jupiter finger.

People with Jupiter fingers that are shorter than their Apollo fingers tend to hold themselves back, and usually feel inadequate and lacking in confidence early on in life. They are often shy and find it hard to reveal much of themselves to others.

As with the other fingers, the phalanges should be approximately equal in length. If the tip phalange is the longest, the person will develop an interest in philosophy or spirituality. This kind of person would work well with other people, especially when placed in a caring or counseling role.

If the middle phalange is the longest, the person will have a practical, intelligent brain, and a positive approach to life. This person will use intellect to come up with good ideas to then carry out. The thinking part of the process will always be the most important aspect for people with a long second phalange on their Jupiter finger.

The base phalange is usually the longest section of the Jupiter finger. This means the person will be involved in the practical aspects of everyday life, and will enjoy keeping busy with a variety of activities. This person will ultimately develop a faith that plays an important role in his or her future life.

Leaning Fingers

Sometimes, people's fingers gain strength from the fingers next to them. This is called "finger cling" or leaning fingers.

If the Mercury (little) finger stands apart from the other fingers, the person will be individualistic and an independent thinker. A natural communicator, this person will probably express him- or herself in an original or even unusual manner. This person will come up with original ideas that can provide new and different solutions to problems.

If the Mercury finger hugs the Apollo (ring) finger, the person will be refined and possess good taste. This person will also express him- or herself in a refined, gentle, and reasonable way. This example of finger cling is different from the little finger that curves slightly toward the third finger. This is known as the "Finger of Sacrifice" and is usually found on the hands of people who care for others. Doctors, nurses, veterinarians, and caregivers of all sorts often have a Finger of Sacrifice on their hands.

Sometimes the Mercury finger will appear to be slightly twisted, and will also curve towards the Apollo finger. This is an indication of someone who will bend the truth when he or she feels it's necessary. This can vary from exaggeration to outright lying.

If the Apollo (ring) finger naturally clings to the Saturn (middle) finger, the person will use his or her creativity to benefit humanity, usually people in the local community. If the Apollo finger possesses a curve towards the Saturn finger, the person will have given up creative aspirations and settled for something less satisfying in order to make a living.

If the Apollo finger curves towards the Mercury finger, the person will subconsciously underrate his or her creative ability. If this person did something creative, it would be better than believed.

The Saturn finger is the finger most likely to curve one way or the other. If it curves over the Apollo finger, the person will subconsciously hold him- or herself back, especially in matters concerning creativity or good taste. This person will also have a tendency to prefer play to hard work.

If the Saturn finger curves towards the Jupiter finger, the person will underrate his or her abilities in all areas of life. In extreme cases, this can lead to an inferiority complex.

If the Jupiter finger naturally stays close to the Saturn finger, the person will prefer to work as part of a group, rather than alone. This is neither good nor bad; it is simply the way this person prefers to operate.

If the Jupiter finger is naturally held away from the Saturn finger, the person will be self-motivated, enthusiastic and have a slightly different approach to life. These people may have unusual occupations, or do everything in their own particular way.

If the Jupiter finger curves towards the Saturn finger, the person will suffer from low self-esteem and lack of confidence. This person will need constant encouragement from friends and family. Someone with this formation will always be happier as second in charge, rather than leader, of any group or organization.

Rings on the Fingers

Rings show that the person desires extra support in the area of life indicated by the finger. Engagement and wedding rings on the Apollo finger do not figure in this, although they proclaim to the world the person's relationship status.

A ring on the Jupiter finger shows the person subconsciously desires more confidence. In extreme cases, this can indicate an inferiority complex or a desire for power over others.

A ring on the Saturn finger helps provide a sense of stability and grounding.

Rings on the Apollo finger that are not engagement or wedding rings indicate someone who is trying to bolster his or her self-image.

A ring on the Mercury finger usually relates to communication, though it is also frequently found on the fingers of sexually adventurous people.

A ring on the thumb shows that the person is seeking inner strength, determination, and willpower.

We have yet to look at the most important finger of all, the thumb. We'll do that in the next chapter.

3

...

THUMBS

Thumbs play an important role in palmistry. In fact, in India, many palmists focus almost entirely on the thumb. I always glance at people's thumbs when first meeting them, as they provide me with a variety of clues about their character.

None of this is surprising as we are the only animals that have an opposing thumb. It was this formation that enabled mankind to progress in the way it did. Chimpanzees are the animals nearest to us, but their thumbs are tiny and primitive in comparison.

Length of the Thumb

The first thing to notice about thumbs is the size. People with long thumbs in proportion to the rest of their hands are usually more ambitious than people with smaller thumbs. Long-thumbed people want to achieve their goals, and are frequently found in leadership roles. Apparently, Napoleon Bonaparte had a very long thumb, and it may well have been this that drove him to the success he enjoyed, at least for a while.

People with short thumbs prefer to be told what to do. They are followers rather than leaders. They find it much harder to achieve their goals than their friends with longer thumbs.

Fortunately, most people have medium-length thumbs. A medium-length thumb reaches approximately a third to halfway up the base phalange of the Jupiter finger. People with medium-length thumbs are able to stand up for themselves when necessary.

Although the thumb appears to have just two phalanges, palmists consider the mound of flesh at the base of the thumb to be a third phalange. The palmistry name for this part of the hand is the mount of Venus, and we'll look at that later.

Willpower and Logic

The phalanges on the fingers should be roughly equal in length (figure 3A). The same principle applies with the thumb. The tip phalange relates to willpower, while the second phalange relates to logic. If the phalanges are equal in length, the person will have an equal amount of willpower and logic. This means the person will be able to come up with good ideas (logic), and then carry them out (willpower).

Most people have more logic than willpower. This means the second phalange is usually longer than the tip phalange.

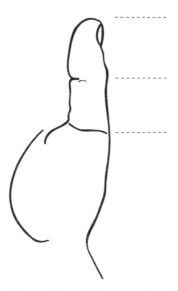

Figure 3A: First and Second Phalanges Equal in Length

When the tip phalange is longer than the second, the person will be full of confidence, energy, and willpower. Acting quickly, this person will make plenty of mistakes along the way but will ultimately achieve his or her goals.

If the logic phalange is longer than the willpower phalange, the person will have a cautious approach to life and will examine all the different options and make detailed plans before acting on them.

If the logic phalange of the thumb is straight and thick, the person will be extremely unwilling to change his or her mind once a decision has been made.

If the logic phalange of the thumb curves inward at its center, making it look like an hourglass, it is called a "waisted phalange." The waisted phalange is called this because it appears to have a waist in the center. People with a waisted second phalange are tactful and diplomatic. They can say "no" in such a nice way that the person they have said it to is halfway down the street before he or she realizes what was actually said.

Setting of the Thumb

Thumbs can be set in different places on the side of the palm. If the thumb is "high-set," it starts well up the hand from the wrist. People with this setting have original ideas and are generally positive and optimistic. They have good self-esteem. If the thumb starts close to the wrist, it is called "low-set." These people are cautious in both their thoughts and actions. Most people possess thumbs that are neither low- nor high-set.

The setting of the thumb has to be considered when determining if the thumb is short, medium, or long. A long thumb that is low-set may only reach a third of the way up the base phalange of the Jupiter finger. Likewise, a medium-length thumb that is high-set might appear long.

Angle of the Thumb

How people hold their thumbs can be a clue to character, too. Most people's thumbs are held at an angle of about forty-five degrees to the hand. These people fit in and conform. They are reasonably open-minded. Some people have an angle that is wider than forty-five degrees. The wider this angle is, the more open, outgoing, and generous the person is. Someone with a wide angle will be adventurous, extroverted, and open to new concepts and ideas. This angle is called the "Angle of Generosity."

Some people have an angle that is considerably less than forty-five degrees. These people are introverted and find it hard to express themselves. In extreme cases, a small angle denotes someone who is selfish, small-minded, and has a limited outlook on life, which seldom sees beyond his or her immediate family.

People who usually hold their thumbs out from their hands are relaxed, positive, outgoing, and happy-go-lucky.

There are two other angles associated with the thumb.

THE ANGLE OF PRACTICALITY

The Angle of Practicality is an angle formed at the base of the logic phalange where it joins the mount of Venus. People with a large angle at this position are practical and enjoy working with their hands. This angle is sometimes also known as the "Angle of Time," as it gives people a special sense of timing. This sometimes, but not always, makes people punctual. It usually gives people a good sense of timing. A good comedian, for instance, who instinctively knows the exact moment to say the punch line of a joke, would have a good Angle of Time. This combination of practicality and timing is useful in sporting activities, and people with this angle are usually good at such activities.

THE ANGLE OF PITCH

The Angle of Pitch is situated at the base of the side of the palm where the thumb joins the wrist. A good angle here gives people a good ear for music and a natural sense of rhythm.

Good musicians, singers and dancers will have good Angles of both Practicality and Pitch. This means they'll possess good timing, from the Angle of Practicality, and a good ear for music from the Angle of Pitch.

Tip of the Thumb

The tip of the thumb is classified in the same way as the fingers.

If the tip of the thumb is square in appearance, the person will have a practical, down-to-earth approach to life. He or she will be fair and easy to get on with.

People with spatulate tips will always be busy and in a hurry. These people will be practical and likely to be good with their hands.

A conic tip indicates a gracious, refined, and sensitive person. Conic tips are frequently found on people who have a "waisted" second phalange. Every now and again, you'll see a tapered tip to the thumb. People with this type of thumb will be deep and subtle thinkers. They can also convey bad news in a caring, sensitive way.

The final type of tip to the thumb is one that is broad and flat. Someone with this tip will be conservative, careful, rigid, and firm.

Related to this is a thumb in which the top phalange appears to be a small knob resting on top of the second phalange. This has the unfortunate title of "Murderer's Thumb." This type of thumb is frequently inherited and I have met a number of families in which most people have this type of thumb. People with a Murderer's Thumb are patient plodders. They achieve their goals after a time. Unfortunately, in domestic situations, people with a Murderer's Thumb can be patient for a long time and then suddenly overreact to a situation with an outburst of temper, often at something trivial. This type of thumb gained its name because of the potential violence that occasionally results from this extreme reaction.

Flexibility

Thumbs are either firm or flexible. If the thumb bends back easily from the joint, it is considered flexible. People with flexible thumbs are easygoing and flexible. They "go with the flow," rather than fight it. They are also inclined to give in under pressure, rather than make a fuss.

If the thumb does not bend back at the joint, it is considered firm. People with stiff, firm thumbs are determined and stubborn. They dig their feet in and do not give in under pressure.

The stiffness of the thumb can be determined by placing one finger on the back of the base phalange, and using your thumb to put gentle pressure on the tip.

The Wheat Line

The Wheat Line is the line that separates the first and second phalanges of the thumb. It is rare for this line to be missing. This is fortunate, as the presence of it shows that the person will always have enough to eat.

This line derives its name because it sometimes contains a small oval, similar to a grain of rice or wheat. This is a sign that the person will lead a happy and fulfilling life.

Sometimes the Wheat Line is made up of two parallel lines. The line starts on the Jupiter finger side of the thumb as a single line, which is joined later by a second parallel line. The second line symbolizes the person's life partner. Consequently, breaks and small crossed lines indicate difficulties in the relationship.

Flower Line

The Flower Line separates the phalange of logic and the mount of Venus. If this line is clear and well marked, the person will enjoy a happy home and family life. This line is frequently in the form of a continual chain. This provides the person with considerable strength of character and moral courage.

Everything we have covered so far concerns the shape of the hands. This is known as *chirognomy*. In the next chapter, we'll start looking at *chirology*, the study of the lines on the palm.

4

...

THE MAIN LINES

FINALLY WE COME TO WHAT most people consider palmistry to be all about: the lines on the palm (figure 4A). There are four main lines, although not everyone has all of them. These lines are usually the most clearly marked lines on the hand. The heart line reveals a person's inner, emotional life. The head line shows how a person thinks. The life line reveals the amount of vitality and energy a person has, and the destiny line shows a person's path through life. These lines should all be clear and well marked on the palm. The stronger each of these lines is, the more energy a person is prepared to put into that area of life.

No one has palms that are exactly alike. Some people have palms that are similar to each other. This person will be doing pretty much what he or she wants to be doing in life. If the palms are totally dissimilar, the person will be thinking about one thing, but doing another. He or she is likely to be constantly frustrated.

The dominant hand, which is the hand the person uses when writing, reveals what the person is doing with his

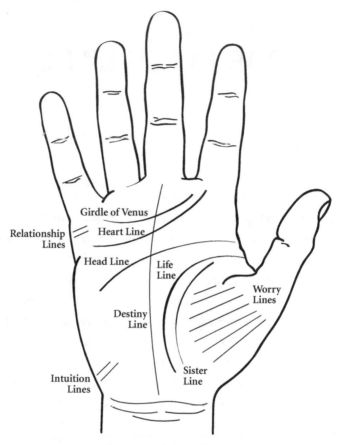

Figure 4A: The Main Lines

or her life. For most people, this is the right hand. The left hand is the dominant hand for left-handers. The less dominant hand, the left hand for right-handers, reveals what the person is thinking about. It also shows inherited traits. This hand is often the more interesting, as it shows what the person would like to be doing, if his or her life was different.

If you are having a quick look at someone's hands, ask to see the right hand if they are right-handed, and the left hand if they are left-handed. If you are doing a complete reading, you'll want to examine both hands.

It's helpful to have a system when reading palms. This ensures you don't accidentally miss anything in your reading. When I look at someone's palms, I start by determining what type of hand they have (fire, earth, air, or water), and then look at the thumb to determine its size and the degree of logic and willpower the person possesses. After this, I look at the four main lines in order. I start with the heart line, and follow this with the head line, life line, and destiny line.

Heart Line

The heart line represents the person's emotional life. It depicts the person's attitudes and responses to love and relationships. The heart line is the major line closest to the fingers. It starts on the Mercury (little) finger side of the palm and usually ends between the Jupiter (index) and Saturn

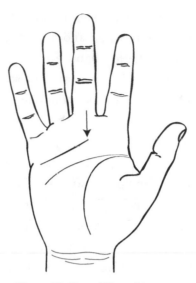

Figure 4B: Mental Heart Line

(middle) fingers. The deeper the heart line is, the more passionate the person's nature is.

The heart line can either run in an almost straight line across the palm, or curve to end almost touching the base of the fingers. These two types of heart lines are known as mental or physical heart lines.

The mental heart line crosses the palm in an almost straight line (figure 4B). Someone with a mental heart line will find it hard to express innermost feelings, particularly early on in life. This person will be sensitive and easily hurt. This person will also need constant reassurance of being loved, and will dislike public displays of affection.

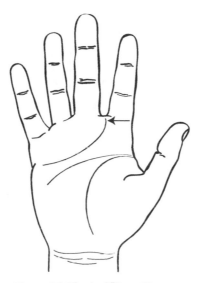

Figure 4C: Physical Heart Line

The curving physical heart line is seen more often than the mental heart line (figure 4C). Someone with a physical heart line will be able to express feelings well. He or she will have an affectionate manner, and have a positive approach to the inevitable ups and downs of life.

The heart line can end under the first finger, between the first and second fingers, or beneath the second finger. The ideal place for it to end is between the first and second fingers (figure 4D). This gives the person a balance between ego (Jupiter finger) and humanity as a whole. These people will have realistic expectations about their emotional lives. This enables these individuals to commit to long-term relationships more easily than people with heart lines that

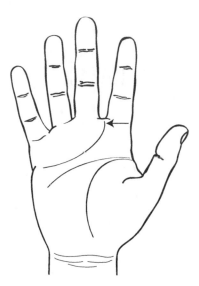

Figure 4D: Heart Line Ending between Jupiter and Saturn Fingers

end in other areas of the palm. This person can also manage to balance personal needs with the needs of others.

If the heart line ends under the first finger, the person will be idealistic and easily hurt (figure 4E). The person will experience a number of emotional disappointments caused by other people failing to live up to impossible expectations. Expressive emotionally, this person will become frustrated with other people who are incapable of expressing themselves in the same way. Someone with a heart line that ends under the first finger will be loyal, faithful, and devoted to the special people in his or her life.

A heart line ending under the second finger indicates one who is concerned mainly with personal gratification

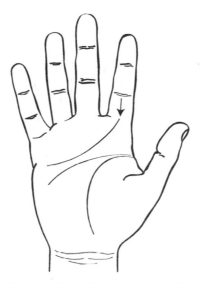

Figure 4E: Heart Line Ending under Jupiter Finger

(figure 4F). Although this person may feel deeply for others, he or she will always make sure that personal needs are met first. This person often displays a lack of emotional involvement but will have strong sexual needs. Frequently, someone with a heart line that ends under the Saturn finger is reserved and finds it difficult to express innermost feelings.

Frequently, a heart line will fork in two or more directions at the end. Two forks give the person the ability to see both sides of a situation. This person will have a complex emotional nature. A trident (three forks) denotes a fortunate life with plenty of emotional energy.

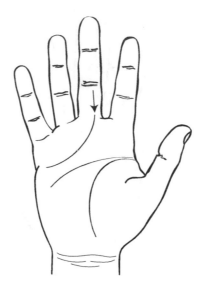

Figure 4F: Heart Line Ending under Saturn Finger

Ideally, the heart line should be clearly marked without any islands or chains present. However, it's rare to find a heart line like this, as we all experience our share of emotional ups and downs as we go through life. Emotional tension is indicated by a series of islands or small ovals inside the line (figure 4G). A group of islands creates a chain-like formation. Timing on the heart line starts from the little finger side of the palm. Consequently, if you meet someone who had an unhappy relationship followed by a happy one, that person would have a number of islands at the start of the line, but the rest of the line would be clear.

Most islands on the heart line are part of a chain. A single island indicates a period of depression or severe emotional stress.

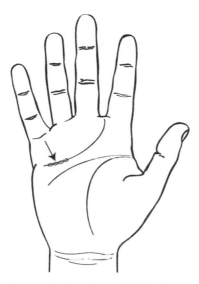

Figure 4G: Heart Line with Islands

Crosses and breaks in the line indicate a major emotional loss and may indicate the end of a relationship.

Sometimes you'll find a fine line paralleling the heart line at the very end. This is a sign that the person will enjoy a long-lasting, happy relationship that is still continuing into old age.

Frequently, you'll find a fine line between the heart line and the fingers. This line is called the Girdle of Venus and is most commonly found on water hands. It is a sign of extreme sensitivity. Consequently, people with it are easily hurt. They also need a great deal of stimulation and variety in their lives. If the Girdle of Venus is made up of a series of small lines paralleling each other, the person will be extremely sensitive, highly emotional, and possibly unstable.

The Head Line

The second line we look at is the head line. Before examining this line, take note of the life line: this is the line that encircles the mount of Venus at the base of the thumb. The head line starts on the thumb side of the palm, between the base of the thumb and the first finger. It either touches or is close to the life line at its start and then comes across the palm, usually paralleling the heart line for part of the way. The head line either crosses the palm in a reasonably straight line or else curves upwards towards the wrist. The length of the head line varies enormously. Some are very short, while others can completely cross the palm. Most head lines fall somewhere between these two extremes and usually finish under the ring finger.

The head line relates to a person's intellect, approach to problem solving, and quality of thinking. At one time, palmists believed that the longer the head line was, the more intelligent the person would be. However, even if that were true—which it isn't—a long head line would not necessarily indicate that the person would use all of the mental ability at his or her disposal. Our brain capacity is unlimited, and no one uses more than a small part of his or her mental potential.

The length of the head line reveals how involved and detailed the person's thinking processes are. Someone with a long head line will think matters through in greater depth than someone with a shorter line. A longer head line means versatility and many interests. If the head line completely crosses the palm, the person will have an inquisitive brain.

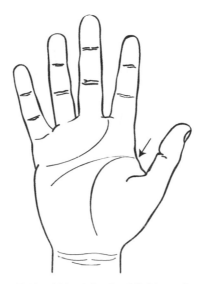

Figure 4H: Head Line Joined to Life Line at Start

This person will want to analyze everything and will possess great insight. Someone with a short head line will think quickly and then act, not wanting to spend too much time analyzing a situation before starting. People with short head lines are shrewd and often do well in business, as they are able to focus on the here and now, and make decisions quickly.

If the head line touches the life line at the start, the person will be cautious and think before acting (figure 4H). If the two lines are close but separated, the person will have a confident approach to life and will enjoy making up his or her own mind on matters concerning life (figure 4I). The farther away the head line is from the life line at the

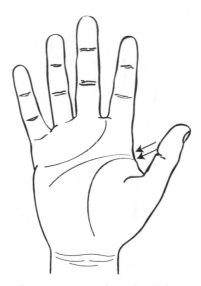

Figure 4I: Head Line Starting Independently from Life Line

start, the more independent the person will be. This person is also likely to be impulsive at times and will also be more open-minded than someone with the head and life lines connected at the start.

There are a few other starting points that you will find from time to time. If the head line starts on the mount of Jupiter (the raised mound at the base of the first finger), the person will be extremely ambitious, and will let nothing get in the way of set goals. If the head line starts inside the life line, the person will be insecure and lacking in confidence. This will relate to the family situation in the early years of the person's life. If the head line starts attached to the life line and remains attached for some

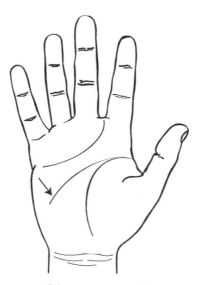

Figure 4J: Imaginative Head Line

distance, the person was unable to make his or her own decisions because of strong family influences.

There are two main types of head lines, known as imaginative and practical head lines. The imaginative head line curves upwards towards the wrist (figure 4J). It ends in a part of the palm known as the creative subconscious. This enhances the person's creativity and imagination. A person with an imaginative head line needs to work in a pleasant environment and to be involved in a career seen as fulfilling and absorbing. This individual will tend to get bored easily and will retreat to his or her excellent imagination when this happens.

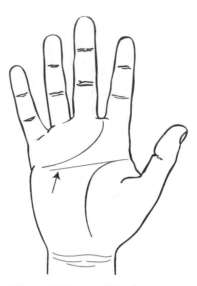

Figure 4K: Practical Head Line

The practical head line runs straight across the palm (figure 4K). People with a practical head line will be level-headed, keep their feet firmly on the ground, and will be happiest in a practical, hands-on type of career that deals with facts. These people will live largely in the real world, and will not spend anywhere near as much time in the fantasy world frequently inhabited by people with imaginative head lines. This doesn't mean these types are unimaginative; it means they have a practical imagination that can quickly assess a situation and then act on it in a direct manner.

Some people have a fork at the end of the head line (figure 4L). One branch will go straight across the palm, while the other branch will curve towards the creative subcon-

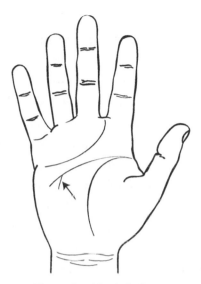

Figure 4L: Writer's Fork

scious. This combination is known as the writer's fork, and it gives the person the advantages of both the imaginative and practical head lines. It shows the person can use imagination to come up with good ideas, and also be practical enough to make them reality. Writers do this every time they come up with a story in their heads and then write it down. This is probably how this fork got its name, but many people who have it have no interest in writing. Anyone who uses his or her imagination and then makes good, practical use of it will be using the writer's fork.

If the head line bends sharply downwards towards the fingers at the very end, the person will have strong material needs, and this will motivate him or her to do well financially. This can be a good thing, but many people with it are impelled by a force within them and don't know when to stop.

Ideally, we want the head line to be clear and unmarked. This shows the person is using his intelligence productively. Chains on the head line indicate stress and tension are affecting the person's ability to think effectively. Chains are frequently found at the start of the head line, especially if it is attached to the life line. This is a sign of tension in the person's home and family life. The chains disappear as the person matures and gains more independence.

An island on the head line indicates stress and confusion. This may be caused because the person is torn between what must be done rather than what he or she would like to do. In rare and extreme cases, this can be a sign of a nervous breakdown.

Breaks in the head line indicate one of two possibilities. It is possible that the brain was not in use at the time indicated by the break. This could indicate that the person was unconscious or suffering from a brain injury. The other possibility is that the person experienced a major change in how he or she felt about life and changed his or her way of thinking. I know a successful artist who spent twenty years working in law enforcement. He experienced a midlife crisis and, much to everyone's surprise, left the force and took up art. This extreme change in his career is clearly revealed by a break in his head line.

The head line should appear strong, vibrant, and well marked. This shows the person is using his or her brain and is enthusiastic and positive about life. If the head line is faint and thin, the person will be a lazy thinker. If the head line is broad and faint, the person will be a slow and sluggish thinker.

Sometimes you'll find a head line that is strong for part of its length, but faint at other times. The strong periods indicate times when the person was forward-looking and decisive, and the faint periods denote periods of boredom or unhappiness.

It can be interesting to compare the head and life lines to see which is the more pronounced line on the hand. Usually, the life line is stronger than the head line. If the head line is the stronger of the two lines, the person's thoughts and inner life will be considered more important than events that occur in real life.

The Simian Crease

Every now and again, the heart and head lines are connected and appear as just the one line. This is known as the simian crease (figure 4M). It's an unfortunate name, insulting to those who have it. It's also incorrect, as monkeys and apes do not possess this line. The simian crease is usually found on one hand. It's rare to find it on both hands. Approximately forty percent of Down's syndrome sufferers have a simian crease. However, most people with it are unafflicted with the syndrome and usually blessed with a high intelligence.

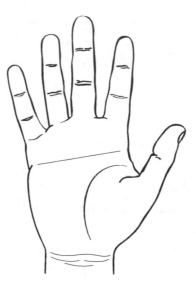

Figure 4M: Simian Crease

People with a simian crease are single-minded and are usually high achievers. Because they are clearly focused on their own goals and desires, they often find it hard to consider the needs of others. They are reasonable until a decision has been made. However, once their minds have been made up, it's extremely hard to get them to consider other options.

If the simian crease is on the dominant hand, the person will possess drive, energy, and ambition. This person will have strong physical appetites and find it hard to relax.

If the simian crease is on the minor hand, the person will dislike responsibility and find it hard to commit. This person is likely to have one absorbing hobby or interest that will be followed with great intensity.

If the simian crease is found on both hands, the person will be obstinate and unyielding, and remain totally unaware of the negative effect these traits can have on others. He or she will be ambitious and will prefer to pursue his or her goals with little input from others.

Life Line

The life line is the line that encircles the thumb. It starts at the edge of the palm on the side of the first finger and forms a semi-circle around the Mount of Venus at the base of the thumb. This line usually starts halfway between the first finger and the base of the thumb. It is a sign of ambition if this line starts closer to the first finger than the thumb. Conversely, it is a sign of lack of ambition if the life line starts close to the base of the thumb.

The life line is the one line that everyone seems to know about. People are fascinated with it, wondering if their life line is as long as it could or should be, and if it predicts when they will die. The length of the line has no bearing on length of life, and the life line on its own does not tell when someone will die. A short life line does not indicate a short life, and a long life line does not indicate a long one. Like the other lines, life lines change over the years and someone with a short life line now may have a long life line in ten years time. Children in particular often have short life lines and parents often ask me about this, as they have noticed their children have life lines that are not as long as theirs.

The life line is the first line to be formed on the palm, and is visible by the time the human embryo is eight weeks old. The heart line is the second line to appear, quickly followed by the head line.

The life line depicts a person's vitality and enthusiasm for life. It also shows how much energy one possesses. Like the other lines, the life line should be clear and well marked. It should also come as far across the palm as possible, as the area it encloses indicates the amount of energy and stamina the person will have. If the life line hugs the thumb, the person will appear half alive and lacking in energy (figure 4N). Conversely, someone with a life line that comes well across the palm will have boundless energy and a much more enthusiastic and positive approach to life (figure 4O).

Some people have what is known as a sister line inside and parallel to the life line (figure 4P). This line is normally found near the start of the life line, but can appear anywhere. It's particularly useful if it's found near the end of the life line, as it has a protective influence. This indicates the person will be physically active late in life. Many years ago, I heard a palmist refer to this line as the "guardian angel" line. It is also known as the line of Mars.

We'll discuss the mount of Venus—the area enclosed by the life line—in chapter seven. Many people have fine lines on this mount that radiate outwards across this mount, starting from the base of the thumb and ending close to, or even crossing, the life line. These are called worry lines, and you'll have no difficulty finding hands with plenty of

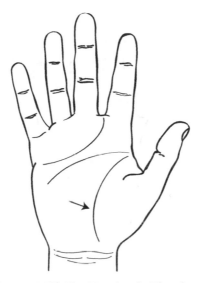

Figure 4N: Life Line Hugging the Thumb

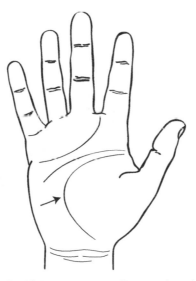

Figure 4O: Life Line Coming Well Across the Palm

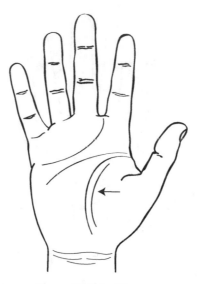

Figure 4P: Sister Line

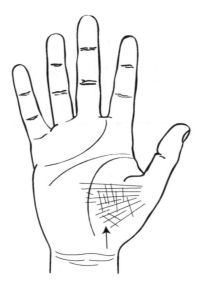

Figure 4Q: Worry Lines

these on them (figure 4Q). Someone with an abundance of worry lines will worry about virtually anything and everything. Someone with just a few worry lines will be concerned and worry only when there's something important to worry about. You'll even find hands with no worry lines on them. Someone with no worry lines will never worry about anything, but you can guarantee his or her partner will have enough worry lines for both of them. It's common for one partner to do most of the worrying in a relationship. Worry lines that cross the life line have the potential to affect the person's health. Whenever I see this, I suggest that the person learn self-hypnosis or meditation to help get their worry under control.

Breaks in the life line are usually not serious, even though they indicate a major change in the person's life at the time indicated. This important change could be almost anything, but it's usually a change in outlook. Most of the time, the life line will overlap itself whenever a break occurs. If the change is a dramatic one such as a relationship breakup, a palmist can frequently determine what it was by looking at other parts of the hand. We'll look at how to synthesize different pieces of information later.

Squares, islands, and chains are the markings most frequently found on the life line. Squares are usually protective, and it's a good sign to see a square enclosing a break in the life line. This shows the person has more than enough energy to resolve the situation. It's not as positive to find a square that covers the life line, but does not enclose a break. This is a sign of confinement. This could mean living in a closed environment, such as a monastery, but is more likely to be a sign of imprisonment. Several years ago, I met a man who had several of these squares on his life line. I discovered that he'd lived on Norfolk Island, a tiny island in the Pacific Ocean, for many years. He said that after a year or so on the island, he'd get "island fever," and would have to get away for a while. Consequently, the confinement squares showed that he felt trapped on the island, even though he was living there by choice.

Islands and chains on the life line both indicate problems. An island is a sign of despondency and possible depression. A chain is a sign of health problems, usually caused by the person's emotional state.

Palmists use the life line to help them time different events. The simplest method is to imagine a line running down the palm from the center of the second (Saturn) finger. Where this line reaches the life line is approximately the age of thirty-five.

The first method I was taught was to measure the length of the life line from where it begins to where it starts to go around the mount of Venus close to the wrist. Where it starts to move around the wrist is said to indicate seventy years. Once you have this measurement, you can work out the time with reasonable accuracy. Half of this length, for instance, would indicate thirty-five. One tenth would be seven years. I have seen palmists in India using this system with a length of thread to measure the line.

Another method divides the life line into three equal sections. Each section indicates approximately twenty to twenty-five years.

A more accurate method involves analyzing marks on the life line to pinpoint events that occurred in the past. If you know the exact time the event occurred, you can use the indication on the line to date future events.

It's important to remember that although the life line can be divided into periods of time, it doesn't reveal the length of the person's life. Someone with a long life line that continues right around the thumb to where the skin patterns end might die at say, thirty years of age, even though his or her life line measured one hundred years. The quality of the line is much more important than its length.

Destiny Line

Now we come to a line that not everyone has: the destiny line, sometimes known as the fate line (figure 4R). I don't like the term "fate line," as it sounds as if life is predetermined and we have no freedom of choice. That certainly is not the case. I know many people who have turned their lives around through their own efforts, and turned failure into success. Such feats would have been impossible if these people had not demonstrated free will and made a conscious decision to change their lives.

The destiny line is a difficult one to describe, as it can start and end in many different places. It usually starts near the wrist and runs down the palm towards the fingers. It can start anywhere near the base of the palm and end anywhere in the palm below the head line. It usually starts somewhere near the center of the palm close to the wrist, and ends under the Saturn (second) finger.

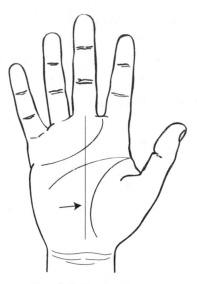

Figure 4R: Destiny Line

Some people have a destiny line that is present for part of its expected length, but it then stops and may or may not start again later. Sometimes the original destiny line will end, and another line will start, parallel to the first.

The mere presence of a destiny line is positive, as it shows that, at least for the time period the line is present, the person will be focused on achieving a goal or dream. Consequently, the destiny line reveals the person's direction in life, his or her capability, and attitude towards life and success.

Old palmistry books say that a long destiny line is a certain indication of success. This is true, as long as the person is motivated to achieve set goals. However, a long destiny line means nothing if the person lacks drive or ambition. I have seen long destiny lines on the hands of many beggars in India. This indicates they have made a lifelong career for themselves as beggars.

It's always a positive sign to see a destiny line in someone's palm. People with destiny lines seem to have luck and good fortune on their side. It's almost as if they are protected from some of the predicaments that people without this line fall into.

It used to puzzle me when I met successful people who had no destiny line on their palms. After all, I had met a number of failures who lacked this line. For some years, I gave talks to prison inmates, and found a large number of them had no destiny line. I've also noticed this in drug addicts and people who take unnecessarily dangerous risks. People without a destiny line take life as it comes. They frequently lead rich and varied lives, but they'll never be consumed by a desire to succeed in a specific field. They will try something for a while and then move on to something else. They may spend their whole lives like a ship without a rudder. Sometimes these people are lucky enough to find a field that proves lucrative. These are the ones who become successful.

If the destiny line starts inside the life line, someone, usually a family member, will have had a strong influence on the person when he or she was growing up. If the destiny line starts away from the life line, close to the center of the hand, the person would have been born with a strong sense of independence. This person will hate restrictions of any sort. This sense of independence increases the farther away from the life line the destiny line is at its start. If it starts more than halfway across the palm, the person is likely to seek a career in the public eye. If the line starts on the small mound on the little finger side of the palm (known as the mount of Luna), the person will have a strong desire to work with others in a creative field. If this person is unable to find enough creativity in a chosen career, a strong creative hobby that will become one of the focuses of this person's life will be developed. This person will also have good social skills and a talent at getting along with virtually everyone.

Someone who was fortunate enough to know exactly what he or she wanted to do in life from an early age will have a destiny line that starts almost on the wrist. If someone starts out in life with no idea what he or she wants to do, and later finds the right career, the destiny line will start at the moment of that discovery. This also occurs if the person suddenly becomes motivated to achieve something with his or her life. Consequently, the destiny line does not necessarily start close to the wrist.

The ending position of a destiny line is important, too. Occasionally, a destiny line will curve slightly and end under the Jupiter (first) finger. This shows the person has an interest in politics, philosophy, and possibly law. Most destiny lines end either under the Saturn (second) finger, or between the Saturn and Apollo (ring) fingers. Someone with a destiny line that ends in this position will follow a conventional type of career. He or she might become a teacher, nurse, or banker, or go into a business or a trade. This person will always choose a relatively usual type of occupation. If the destiny line ends under the Apollo (ring) finger, the person will be engaged in some sort of creative activity. He or she might become an artist, musician, or interior decorator. It's also possible that this person works in an aesthetic field that provides opportunities for creative touches. It's possible, but unusual, for a destiny line to curve and end under the Mercury (little) finger. Someone with this ending position will be involved in a career that utilizes communication skills. This could be anything, ranging from an entertainer to a born salesperson.

Every now and again, you'll see a destiny line that ends with three small branches, creating a trident. This indicates someone who thoroughly enjoys life, and is able to successfully combine duty and pleasure.

Some people have more than one destiny line. The main destiny line will be stronger than the second line, which is found on the thumb side of the main destiny line. This is a sign that the person is doing two or more important activities at one time. This could be, for instance, running a business while also being involved in local politics. It might be a career and an important hobby. It can even indicate someone who needs a great deal of variety in life, and consequently spells out involvement in a wide range of interests.

Breaks are commonly found on the destiny line. They are indications of a change of career if the line stops, but another line starts to one side of it. Usually, the two lines will overlap slightly. This shows the period during which the person thought about the upcoming change.

Squares always serve a protective function on the destiny line. They effectively protect the person whenever necessary.

Many people have a small line that crosses the destiny line in the area between the head and heart lines. The space between these two lines is called the quadrangle. This line normally runs between the head and heart lines, and crosses the destiny line. This cross formation is usually frustrating. It indicates ultimate success, but eventually, as it comes after a variety of delays, setbacks, and other frustrations.

You can time events on the destiny line. The first thirty-five years of the person's life are revealed in the line from the wrist to where it crosses the head line. The ages thirty-six to forty-nine are shown in the quadrangle, the area between the head and heart lines. The rest of the person's life is shown in the area between the heart line and the fingers. This may seem strange, as more than half of the destiny line covers the first thirty-five years.

There is a reason for this. In palmistry, the first thirty-five years are essentially the preparation years. By the age of thirty-five, most people have worked out what they want to do with their lives. They may have made a few false starts, indicated by breaks in the destiny line.

The destiny line usually follows a direct path between thirty-six and forty-nine. Most people are following a set path at this stage, and are probably in a stable relationship and progressing in their career. Of course, this doesn't apply to everyone, and any changes that occur at this time will be shown in the destiny line.

For many people, the destiny line stops at the heart line. This is the start of middle age in palmistry, and is a time when many people gradually become set in their ways. It doesn't mean their destiny stops at the age of forty-nine. If the destiny line carries on after the heart line, the person will be engaged in new and different activities after the age of forty-nine. This is sometimes an indication of longevity. It often means that the person has no desire to retire and keeps on working until his or her death.

5
...

EXAMINING
THE HAND

IN ADDITION TO THE SHAPE of the hand and the lines on the palm, there are a number of other things that need to be examined. Most of these can be determined with a glance.

Handshake

People who are open and friendly shake hands with a reasonably firm handshake. If the handshake feels like an attempt to crush your hand, the person is concealing his or her insecurities by trying to dominate you.

Some people offer you a limp hand to shake. My mother called this a "wet-fish" handshake, and believed these people were reluctant to meet anyone new. This sort of handshake is off-putting and unpleasant to receive. However, the traditional interpretation is not always correct. People who shake hands all the time such as celebrities and politicians sometimes adopt a "wet-fish" handshake to protect their hand from potential bone crushing handshakes.

How the Hand Is Held

When someone shows you their palms for a reading, the fingers will be displayed either held together or apart. Someone who shows you his or her hands with the fingers and thumb held together will be cautious, and possibly lacking in confidence. Someone who displays his or her hands with the fingers spread apart will be more confident, self-assured, and generous.

Some people are naturally closed all the time. These people are very difficult to get to know in the first place, and even after knowing them for many years, they still reveal little about themselves. These people hold their hands with the thumb touching one of the other fingers

Sometimes you'll find someone who gradually closes his or her hands as you're examining them. This shows that he or she is concerned you'll discover his or her deepest secrets.

Consistency

Some people have palms that are well padded, and may feel soft and spongy to the touch. People with hands of this type enjoy indulging and spoiling themselves. They enjoy all the luxuries that life has to offer. They are adaptable and usually dependent on someone else to earn the necessary money to support their lifestyle.

People with hands that feel hard to the touch enjoy the occasional luxury, but do not crave them in the same way that people with fleshy palms do. They need to be busy to be happy. They enjoy physical activity. People with hard palms are resilient and make the best of any situation they find themselves in, but they find it hard to adjust when conditions change.

Most people have palms that are neither hard nor spongy. Their hands are firm, but yield to pressure.

Moist and Dry Hands

Most people have slightly moist hands on extremely hot days, but it means something if the hand is clammy in normal temperatures. A damp hand indicates nervousness and anxiety. It can sometimes indicate emotional problems too.

Skin Texture

The pores in the skin are obvious in people with coarse hands. The pores are hard to see in a refined hand. It is usually easier to determine if someone has a refined or coarse hand by looking at the back of the hand.

People with coarse hands have basic needs and appetites. As long as these are satisfied, they're happy. These people enjoy spending time with like-minded friends, and tend to overindulge whenever the opportunity arises. They find it hard to express their innermost feelings, and usually prefer action to words. They are down-to-earth, practical, and thick-skinned. Coarse hands are found most frequently on people with earth hands.

People with refined hands are more cultured and aesthetic. They like their home and work environments to be attractive and reflect their good taste.

You will sometimes find an extreme version of the refined hand. If you run a finger over the palm of this type of hand you'll be unable to feel any of the lines or other skin ridge patterns on the palm. This reveals someone who is extremely sensitive and fastidious. This extreme version of the refined hand is found most commonly on people with water hands, and it increases the intuitive aspect of their natures.

This extreme version of the refined hand is also revealed by a fine, smooth skin texture on the back of the hand. This is a sign of femininity, and is rarely seen on a man's hand.

Hair

A small amount of hair on the back of a man's hand is desirable as it denotes masculinity. A large amount of hair is less desirable as it reveals someone with large physical appetites who will do whatever is necessary to satisfy them.

Fingernails

While examining the hand, check the condition of the fingernails. Someone who looks after him- or herself will have well tended fingernails. Dirty and broken fingernails might be a result of the work the person does. It may reveal a keen gardener. However, it may also indicate a slovenly person who pays no attention to appearance.

Practical people keep their fingernails reasonably short. The longer the fingernails are, the less practical the person will be. I once saw a man who had allowed the fingernail on his right forefinger to grow about twelve inches in length. It looked like a rather dirty corkscrew, as the nail spiraled as it grew. It was unsightly and made it impossible for him to undertake many normal, everyday activities.

Color

The color of the palms helps reveal the person's health and temperament. Naturally, this can only be determined under normal room temperature. It would be unusual, for instance, to find someone who had just come in from a long walk in the snow to have pink hands.

People with naturally white hands are inclined to be anemic, and lacking in energy. They are short-tempered, irritable, and cold.

People with yellowish hands have a slightly jaundiced view of life. Bluish hands indicate the person's blood circulation is poor.

Pinkish hands, in people of European descent, are considered normal and people with them are loving, sympathetic, and considerate.

Red hands reveal someone with a great deal of energy. If this energy is not directed wisely, the person is likely to be bad tempered. Sometimes the redness can be seen on only part of the hand. This increases the energies of that particular part of the hand.

Flexibility

You can test the flexibility of someone's hands by resting the back of their palms on your fingers while using your thumb to press downwards on the palm side of their fingers. If the person is flexible in outlook, his or her fingers will move backwards easily. If the person has a rigid approach to life, the fingers will appear stiff and unyielding.

Now that we've looked at hand shapes, texture, flexibility, and the four major lines, you know enough to give someone a quick reading. We'll do that in the next chapter.

6

...

HOW TO GIVE A
BRIEF PALM READING

IF YOU ARE GOING TO take up palmistry seriously, you should look at as many hands as possible. Many people starting out in palmistry find this hard to do as they're aware that they're still beginners and will be unable to answer people's questions. For many people this becomes a catch-22 type of situation but it's an essential part of the process. If you look at as many hands as possible, you'll learn the basics of palmistry much more quickly.

The best way to start giving readings is to tell people that you're studying palmistry but are still learning. You'll find almost everyone will want to show you their palms.

Start by looking at the dominant hand. This is the person's right hand if he or she is right handed, and the left if left handed. Some people are ambidextrous. This means they can use either hand equally well. I used to hate playing tennis with my brother, as instead of playing a backhand, he'd move his racquet from one hand to the other.

If someone is ambidextrous, ask the person to interlock his or her fingers. Note which thumb is on top, as it belongs to the person's dominant hand.

Start by looking at one area. It's a good idea to begin with the hand shapes: fire, earth, air, and water. With most people it will be a simple matter to determine what type of hands they have. However, you'll find exceptions. Is it an air or earth hand if the person has a square palm and medium-length fingers? As the person knows you're a student of the subject, you'll be able to ask him or her questions to determine which classification is correct.

Once you've become adept at determining hand shapes, study people's thumbs. Keep looking at hand shapes, of course, but start looking at the thumbs as well. Are they large or small? High set or low? Is the phalange of will longer or shorter than the phalange of logic? Does the person have the waisted second phalange that indicates tact and diplomacy?

After this, you might like to look at the Jupiter (index) finger, followed by the other fingers. Ask as many questions as you can, as people's answers will help you understand the fundamentals of palmistry.

Look at the lines of the hand individually. You might start with the life line, as that is the one you'll receive the most questions about. Does this line come well out across the palm, or does it hug the thumb? Are there any breaks or other markings on the line? Does the person have a sister line inside the life line? Are there many worry lines? Experiment with the different methods of timing.

By looking at hands in this way, you'll quickly learn the basics without needing to study and memorize each detail. Once someone tells you what a specific shape, line, or mark on the hand means, you'll remember it forever.

By the time you've completed this exercise, you'll have discovered, if you hadn't before, that everyone's hands are different. I find hands fascinating. More than once, my wife has told me, "Stop it!" when we've been at parties. This is because I've been looking at people's hands more than their faces.

When looking at people's hands, the golden rule is: be gentle. Choose your words carefully, as the people you read for will remember everything you say. This is the case even when people apparently consider the reading is purely for laughs.

Let's look at a sample hand. We'll assume the hand is:

- An air hand.
- The hand is flexible, and the thumb is firm.
- The thumb is large, and the phalanges of logic and willpower are equal in length.
- The thumb is high set. It also creates a ninety degree angle when it is held open.
- The Apollo (ring) finger is slightly longer than the Jupiter (index) finger.
- The Mercury (little) finger is low-set.
- The heart line is a physical heart line, which ends between the first and second fingers. There is a fork at the end of the line.

- The head and life lines are connected at the start.
- The head line is an almost straight line that almost crosses the palm. It has a well marked writer's fork.
- The life line comes well across the palm and curves around the wrist. There are no breaks or marks on the line.
- There is a reasonable number of worry lines.
- The destiny line starts close to the wrist, in the center of the palm, well away from the life line. It has a change of direction, indicated by one line ending, and another one starting, in the person's early thirties. The destiny line ends under the second finger.
- The destiny line is crossed in the area between the head and heart lines.

We'll assume this hand belongs to a forty-four-year-old man. What would you say to him as you looked at his palm? Please try this yourself before reading further.

I might say to this person: "You have a good strong hand. You're capable, versatile, and have an extremely active mind. You enjoy mental challenges. You're a deep thinker and you express yourself well when you choose to. You're well balanced and emotionally stable (air hand).

"You're ambitious and prepared to work hard to achieve your goals. You can come up with good ideas, and then carry them out (large thumbs with logic and willpower even in size). You're usually positive and optimistic, and enjoy looking ahead (high set thumb). You're open, outgoing and generous (ninety-degree angle of the thumb).

"Your fingers are well balanced. You have what's known as a 'dropped' little finger. This means that everything goes well for you for a long time, and then you'll experience a setback or disappointment. Fortunately, you're a positive person and bounce back quickly. At times, you've had to learn the hard way. You might have been shy in your younger years (Mercury finger). You can stand up for yourself, when necessary (strong thumb).

"You definitely have more confidence now than you used to. You might have held yourself back early on in life (Apollo finger longer than Jupiter finger).

"You have a strong heart line that ends in the perfect place, between these two fingers. It's what's known as a physical heart line, and that means you can express your innermost feelings without too much difficulty. The fork at the end of this line complicates your emotional life at times, but it also enables you to see both sides of a given situation (heart line).

"You have a long head line. This makes you a good thinker, and you like to work things out for yourself. You're a practical thinker. You're interested in all sorts of things, and want to learn as much as you can about them. You don't get carried away, though. You generally keep your feet firmly on the ground. You're good with details, and whatever work you do should be as involved as possible (head line). You're cautious, and think before you act (head and life line joined at start). You have what is known as a writer's fork, which gives you the ability to think up good ideas and the ability to make them happen. It gives a creative slant to your brain (Writer's fork).

"You have a strong, clear, well-marked life line. This shows you have a great deal of energy and stamina, as well as vitality and enthusiasm. If you were doing something you enjoyed, you'd be able to keep on doing it almost indefinitely (life line). You worry at times, usually when there's cause for it. None of these cross your life line, so worry is not likely to affect your health (worry lines).

"You've always seen yourself as an independent person. It looks as if you had a good idea of what you wanted to do in life from an early age. Your destiny line is strong and direct. It ends under this finger (Saturn finger), which shows you've chosen a standard type of career path for yourself. There was a major change of direction in your early thirties. As it's on your destiny line, I assume this was a major change in your career. As the line continues on in a direct manner, the change was obviously a good one (destiny line). Although your destiny line is a good, strong line, your life hasn't always progressed as quickly or as easily as you might have liked. You've had your share of delays and setbacks. It's been frustrating at times. Fortunately, this cross is a sign of ultimate success, so you will achieve your goals (cross in the quadrangle)."

Isn't it amazing how much information you can give someone with what we've already covered? In this quick reading, we completely ignored the finger phalanges and markings on the major lines. Despite that, we've given this man a great deal of information about himself.

In the next chapter, we'll look at the mounts on the palms.

7

...

THE MOUNTS

THE MOUNTS ARE SMALL MOUNDS on the surface of the palm (figure 7A). They are normally unnoticeable, but they still play an important role in palmistry as they reveal the person's natural strengths and talents. Mounts show what a person enjoys doing and how much energy the person is prepared to put into that activity or activities. If the person has not already discovered them, the mounts can reveal hidden talents. The mounts are often used when the palm reader is doing vocational analysis. Naturally, people are happiest at work when they're involved in activities they enjoy.

There are nine mounts on the palm. The large mound at the base of the thumb encircled by the life line is the mount of Venus. Directly across the palm from the mount of Venus on the little finger side, close to the wrist is the mount of Luna. Between the mounts of Luna and Venus, at the base of the palm close to the wrist, is a small mound called the mount of Neptune. There are also mounds under each finger, and they have the same traditional names

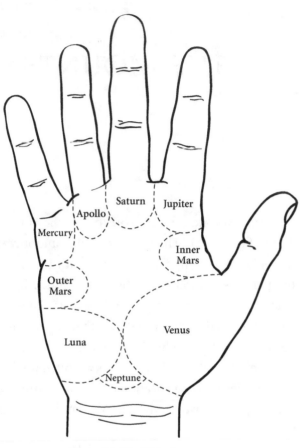

Figure 7A: The Mounts

the fingers do. The mount of Jupiter is situated immediately below the Jupiter (index) finger. The mount of Saturn is directly below the Saturn (second) finger. The mount of Apollo is immediately below the Apollo (ring) finger, and the mount of Mercury is directly below the Mercury (little) finger. The final two mounts are the mounts of Mars. The inner mount of Mars is situated on the thumb side of the palm between the mount of Venus and the mount of Jupiter. The outer mount of Mars is situated on the little finger side of the palm between the mount of Mercury and the mount of Luna.

The mounts are complicated because some people appear to have no mounts, some people seem to have all of them, while others appear to have just some of them. In actuality, everyone has all nine mounts, even though they may not be clearly visible. If you find it hard to see the mounts in your own palm, hold your palm horizontally in front of you with the fingers touching each other. You might have to tilt the palm downwards slightly to see the mounts. The mounts beneath your fingers will be the most visible. They may lie between the fingers, rather than directly under them.

Ideally, we want the mounts to be high, wide, and firm. A high mount shows the person will be active and energetic in the areas indicated by the mount. This is physical activity. A wide mount shows the person will put thought into the area indicated by the mount. This is mental activity. If the mount is firm, the person will be using the related knowledge he or she has gained. A soft, spongy mount shows that the person has gained the knowledge, but isn't using it. A mount that is neither firm nor spongy shows the person will use the qualities of the mount in a gentle, caring way.

With most people, one mount will predominate over the others. This reveals the person's main area of interest. Occasionally, you'll find a hand in which all the mounts are equally strong. This is said to be a "lucky hand," because the owner of it will have plenty of drive and ambition, as well as the necessary confidence, to achieve his or her goals.

You will also find hands in which it is hard to determine any of the mounts. Someone with a hand like that will be lacking in confidence and doubt his or her ability to achieve anything in life. If this hand feels firm, the person will be able to set and achieve goals but will find it much harder to achieve them than someone with high, wide, and firm mounts.

The Mount of Venus

We'll start with the mount of Venus, as that is the easiest mount to identify. The mount of Venus is the mound at the base of the thumb that is encircled by the life line. This mount relates to love, passion, vitality, sympathy, and empathy.

This mount should be reasonably high and firm. This denotes someone who is sympathetic, affectionate, sociable, and fun to be with. He or she will possess a strong aesthetic sense, and will enjoy being inside a strong, supportive, close, loving relationship. This person will also be energetic, enthusiastic, and passionate.

The higher this mount is, the greater the degree of physical passion. Because of this, the mounts of Venus of any two people involved should be examined when determining compatibility. Obviously, a couple will have problems if one partner has a large, high mount of Venus, and the other has a flat, or even inverted, mount of Venus. Once a night would not be enough for one, whilst once a decade would be far too much for the other.

Sadly, you will see flat and inverted mounts of Venus at times. These people are likely to be lonely, as they lack compassion, love, and sympathy. They are frigid and have little or no interest in sex. They find it hard to express their innermost feelings to others. However, they frequently lead a rich, secret, inner life and often possess a strong intuitive sense.

The breadth of this mount is determined by the curve of the life line. If the life line comes well out across the palm, the person will be friendly, warm, and enthusiastic. He or she will also be generous in love.

The Finger Mounts

There is a mount beneath each finger. If you use a magnifying glass, you'll be able to find the triangular skin ridge patterns that indicate the center of these mounts. The importance of these mounts is increased if the apex (center) of the mount is situated directly under the finger. This is comparatively rare, though; most finger mounts are displaced to one side or other, and are not sited directly under the finger. When this occurs, the mount tends to take on some of the qualities of the finger it is displaced towards in addition to the basic qualities of the mount.

THE MOUNT OF JUPITER

The mount of Jupiter is found at the base of the first finger. If this mount is high, wide, firm, and well sited, the person will be a natural leader, and people will look to him or her to take charge in all kinds of situations. A strong Jupiter mount is found on the hands of many influential people, as it reveals intelligence, initiative, ambition, and good self-esteem. As the Jupiter mount sometimes relates to philosophy and religion, many charismatic religious leaders also possess a strong Jupiter mount.

If this mount is high, but feels spongy, the person will be proud, vain, and have a strong sense of his or her own self-importance. This person will enjoy showing off, and will overindulge whenever the opportunity presents itself.

If the mount of Jupiter is displaced towards the edge of the palm, the person will be egotistical. If it is displaced towards the Saturn (second) finger, the person will be self-conscious, but will gain some of the positive Saturnine qualities such as thoughtfulness and wisdom. He or she will work well as part of a team, and will not have the strong desire for praise and appreciation that most people with strong mounts of Jupiter require.

It is a sign of a lack of confidence if the mount of Jupiter appears flat. This person will always be happy to sit back and let other people take charge.

THE MOUNT OF SATURN

This mount is found at the base of the second finger. Most people have a flat, rather than a raised, Saturn mount. This is fortunate, as Saturn was a rather gloomy god and a high, wide, and firm mount of Saturn creates a distinctly Saturnine person. This individual will be a hard worker but will prefer to work alone rather than as part of a group or team. This person will enjoy challenging work, especially if it is detailed and involved. He or she will also have strong feelings but find it hard to express love and affection to others. If this mount is the dominant mount on the hand, the person's greatest pleasures in life will revolve around home and family. This person will have a strong sense of duty that often leads to him or her taking on much more than his or her fair share of a project.

People with a flat mount of Saturn avoid all the negative aspects of this mount.

If the mount of Saturn is displaced towards the Jupiter (index) finger, the person will gain the positive Jupiter qualities of optimism and confidence. If this mount is displaced towards the Apollo (ring) finger, the person will gain a more positive approach to life, but will still need considerable time away from others.

THE MOUNT OF APOLLO

The mount of Apollo is found at the base of the ring finger. It is an important mount as it influences the person's outlook on beauty, creativity, happiness, and success.

A high, firm, and wide mount of Apollo provides the person with enthusiasm, a strong sense of beauty, and the ability to get along well with others. These people will be adaptable, charming, and persuasive. They will also possess good taste and appreciate beauty in all its forms. This person will also be shrewd with money and good at evaluating moneymaking opportunities.

Not surprisingly, there are also a few negative traits if the mount of Apollo is overdeveloped. The person may be quick tempered and prone to sudden outbursts of anger. Vanity, ostentatiousness, and a tendency to exaggerate to make good stories better are also possible.

If the mount of Apollo is soft and spongy, the person will dream about achieving success, but will lack the necessary motivation to achieve it. He or she could dabble in creative fields but never quite get around to developing his or her talent further.

Some people have no visible mount of Apollo. This denotes individuals who are practical and down-to-earth, but lacking in imagination. These folks will have little interest in creative activities and will have no desire to decorate their homes with attractive items.

It is common for this mount to be displaced towards the Saturn or Mercury fingers. If the mount of Apollo is sited partway towards the Saturn finger, the person will be creative, but will prefer to compose music or write plays rather than stand up and perform. This person will also relate well to young people and would do well in a career that deals with children.

The performing aspect comes out if the mount of Apollo is displaced toward the Mercury finger. This person will enjoy producing, directing, and performing. As he or she will also be astute financially, this person may become involved in the business side of the arts, promoting creative activities to the world. This person is also likely to have a special affinity with animals.

THE MOUNT OF MERCURY

The mount of Mercury is situated at the base of the little finger. A well-developed mount of Mercury is found on the hand of someone with a good brain and, because this mount relates strongly to communication, the ability to express thoughts clearly. This person will be a quick thinker and enjoy mental challenges. Consequently, a prominent mount of Mercury is often found on the hands of teachers, debaters, and actors. This person will be affectionate and easy to get on with. Home and family life will also be important.

If this mount is overdeveloped, the person will stretch the truth by telling others what they want to hear. Someone with an overdeveloped mount of Mercury will be unreliable, because promises might not be kept or be forgotten altogether.

Someone with an undeveloped mount of Mercury will be impractical, insincere, and lack good communication skills. This person is likely to be full of big ideas, but have no motivation to achieve them.

The mount of Mercury is frequently sited towards the Apollo (ring) finger. This gives the person a cheerful, positive, carefree approach to life. It is unusual for the mount of Mercury to be displaced towards the edge of the palm. This shows the person will display great courage when necessary.

Sometimes the mounts of Mercury and Apollo seem to form one large mount. This person will be highly creative and have a wide range of interests.

The Mounts of Mars

The two mounts of Mars are situated opposite each other on the palm of the hand. The mount of Venus is situated inside the life line on the finger side of the base of the thumb. The fold of flesh that moves if you extend your hand and move your thumb slightly is the inner mount of Mars. It is sited between the mounts of Jupiter and Venus. The inner mount of Mars relates to courage and the ability to stand up for oneself. It should be firm. If it's too hard, the person will be aggressive and quick to take offense. If it's soft, spongy, and undeveloped, the person will find it hard to stick up for him- or herself.

The outer mount of Mars relates to integrity and moral courage. It is situated between the heart and head lines on the little finger side of the palm. The head line may finish on the outer mount of Mars, but the heart line is always outside the mount. A strong outer mount of Mars gives the person the ability to hang on, long after other people have given up. It gives the person self-control.

A weak outer mount of Mars is flat, soft, and spongy. Again, someone with this finds it hard to stand up to others and is easily overcome by those who are more powerful and dominant.

Strong mounts of Mars are essential for people involved in competitive sports, as it gives them the necessary desire, energy, motivation, persistence, and aggression.

If one or both of the mounts of Mars are strong the person will be generous and hospitable. These people value friendship and are prepared to stick up for their friends whenever necessary.

The Plain of Mars

The area between the two mounts of Mars is called the plain of Mars. Like the mounts, it should be firm to the touch. It enables the person with this quality to make good, positive use of the energies provided by the lines that cross this area. These include the important heart, head, and destiny lines.

If the plain of Mars is thick, firm, and hard, the person will be full of his or her own self-importance and will tend to ignore other people's feelings.

If the plain of Mars is soft and spongy, the person will be easily led, lack confidence, and make more than his or her share of mistakes. A soft plain of Mars is often found on the hands of teenagers. Fortunately, this area often firms up as the person matures. People with a soft plain of Mars are usually shy.

The Mount of Luna

The mount of Luna lies at the base of the little finger side of the hand directly opposite the thumb. It governs the creative subconscious and indicates the person's imagination, creativity, and emotional nature. It relates strongly to dreams and intuitions. This mount should be firm to the touch, and have a well-defined apex on it. The apex is a skin ridge pattern similar to fingerprints. We'll look at them in chapter nine.

People with a well-developed mount of Luna will have a good imagination and a strong appreciation of beauty. These individuals will express compassion to all living things.

If the mount of Luna is the dominant mount on the hand, the person will be sensitive and prefer daydreaming to life in the real world. This person will live in a fantasy world and lack the necessary drive to achieve goals. If this is the dominant mount on a man's hand, he is likely to be effeminate. A woman is likely to be frivolous and superficial if this is the dominant mount on her hand.

If the mount of Luna is flat, the person will have little imagination and will keep his or her feet firmly on the ground.

The Mount of Neptune

The mount of Neptune is situated at the base of the hand by the wrist, between the mounts of Luna and Venus. When this mount is firm, it creates a level surface on the palm where the three mounts meet.

A strong mount of Neptune gives one the ability to think quickly on one's feet. It is found on the hands of public speakers and anyone who performs in public.

If this mount is underdeveloped, the person will find it hard to express innermost feelings.

———————

As you can see, the mounts provide a wealth of information about the owner of the hands. In the next chapter, we'll add to everything we've covered so far by discovering how revealing the minor lines on the palm can be.

THE MINOR LINES

THE HAND SHAPES, FINGERS, THUMB, major lines, and mounts are the most important factors in palmistry. However, the minor lines also need to be examined as they'll help you answer the many questions you'll receive from people you read for.

As a palmist, you'll be amazed how often you'll hear: "Will I get married?" "Will I travel?" "How many children will I have?" "Will I succeed in my career?" "How is my health?" You'll be able to gain insight into all these questions, and many more, by looking at the minor lines on the hand. Consequently, although these lines are called "minor lines," they are just as important as the major lines when it comes to reading the hand.

You will not find all of these lines in every hand. Most people have some of the minor lines, but it's relatively unusual to find someone who has all of them on his or her palm.

The Health Line (Hepatica)

The health line is usually called the hepatica, which comes from the Latin *hepaticus*, which means the liver (figure 8A). The hepatica is also sometimes referred to as the line of Mercury or the liver line. The health line runs diagonally across the palm from close to, or even inside, the life line near the wrist to somewhere near the start of the heart line. The absence of a health line is a good sign. Someone without a health line will enjoy excellent health, and will usually manage to avoid seasonal illnesses, such as colds and the flu. Someone without a health line usually leads a life free of stress.

If the health line is present, it should be as well marked and as clear as possible. This shows that the person looks after him- or herself and enjoys good health.

A long, straight, clear health line that crosses the palm and ends on the mount of Mercury is a sign of longevity. This person will look after his or her health, and manage to reach an advanced age with few health problems.

If the health line varies in quality, the person will experience ill health at times. This does not necessarily indicate a specific illness.

Health problems are indicated by islands, breaks, and periods when the line is faint. The timing of these events is often revealed in the life line. Islands frequently indicate problems with the digestive system, and a change of diet sometimes affects the quality of the health line. Breaks in the line indicate periods of ill health. A square on the

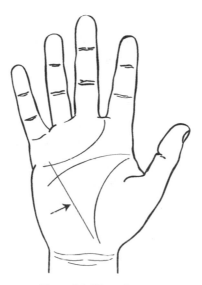

Figure 8A: Hepatica

health line protects the person for the period indicated. It is an extremely positive sign that indicates the person will make a complete recovery from the health concern.

The Sun Line

The sun line is a fortunate line to possess as it gives one a sunny disposition and the potential for great success in a chosen career. William Benham, a famous palmist of the early twentieth century, called the sun line the "line of capability,"[1] as he believed everyone who had it was capable of great achievement in their careers. Certainly, people who possess it are able to discard the thousands of extraneous thoughts we all have every day, and focus intently on their goals. It may well be this ability that leads them to success.

The sun line parallels the destiny line for part of its length. In exceptional people, this line starts close to the wrist and finishes near the Apollo (ring) finger. Consequently, it is sometimes called the line of Apollo. However, it's rare to see a sun line of that length. Usually, the sun line starts near the head line and runs towards the third finger. Sometimes you'll see a sun line that starts close to the wrist, but is very short. This shows the person made an exceptional start to his or her career, but was unable to sustain it.

It is rare to find a long, clear, unmarked sun line. This indicates a successful career, free of obstacles and difficulties. Life tends to create problems at times for everyone, and even the most fortunate people experience their share of ups and downs. Consequently, you're likely to find islands, breaks, and other markings on virtually every sun line you see.

An island on the sun line indicates a sudden loss of reputation. Most people who have a sun line are honest and ethical, but someone who is a successful criminal may also possess a sun line, denoting a successful life in crime. Oftentimes an island indicates a scandal of some sort, or some secret from the person's private life affecting his or her career.

A cross on the sun line indicates a financial setback. If the line continues on beyond the cross, the person will be able to recover from this loss and continue on the career path.

A break in the sun line indicates a period in which the individual is not fully appreciated or recognized for efforts made. Many breaks indicate someone who is a dilettante: extremely talented and versatile but easily bored, with the tendency to lose interest in different activities just as they are about to bear fruit.

A square on the sun line protects the person's good name and reputation. It offers protection against jealousy, slander, and attempts to bring one down to size.

The Line of Mars

The line of Mars is a short line that starts between the life line and the thumb and curves onto the mount of Venus. It is sometimes confused with the sister line that protects the life line. However, the line of Mars is more pronounced than a sister line, and curves around the mount of Venus, rather than hugging the life line.

The line of Mars is a sign of excellent health, and the ability to recuperate quickly after an illness. It provides energy and vitality. Traditionally, the presence of the line of Mars was a sign that the person possessed a talent of some sort. You need to examine the rest of the palm to determine what the particular talent is.

Travel Lines

Travel lines are shown as fine lines on the little finger side of the palm that rise up into the mounts of Luna and outer Mars. Some people's travel lines appear all the way down the side of the palm to the start of the heart line.

Not everyone has travel lines. This doesn't mean that people without travel lines don't travel. It simply means they have less interest in traveling than people with many travel lines. Some people have dozens of travel lines. Each line does not indicate a trip somewhere. It shows that they think about travel a great deal. In fact, if circumstances conspire against them, some of these people could travel less than some people who have no travel lines. Most people with travel lines manage to travel every now and again, as the lines indicate a strong need to travel and broaden horizons. People who work in the travel industry are likely to have a number of travel lines on their hands per their interest in travel. However, every single trip one takes will not show up as a travel line, especially if most of the travel is for work rather than pleasure. Important travel is usually indicated by stronger lines: usually the first overseas trip someone takes shows up as a strong line.

Longer travel lines usually indicate more extensive travel than short lines. A long line might indicate a lengthy European vacation, for instance, while a short line might indicate a weekend in San Francisco. However, there are exceptions. Someone who lives in a small village and visits a large city once in his life would have a long, clear travel line, as this trip was extremely important to him. Consequently, longer lines can indicate important travel as well as extensive travel.

A square on a travel line shows that the person will be protected on that particular trip. An island on this line indicates some sort of loss during the trip. The most likely loss is money, but it could also indicate the ending of a friendship. A cross on a travel line is a sign of disappointment, showing that the travel did not live up to the person's expectations.

Travel lines are sometimes called restlessness lines. This is a better name for them, as travel is one way of satisfying needs for freedom and variety.

The Ring of Solomon

The Ring of Solomon is a fine semi-circular line beneath the Jupiter (index) finger. This usually gives the person a strong interest in psychic matters. However, people who possess it may or may not consider themselves psychic. Many people with this ring subconsciously use their intuition to assess and understand other people. If someone has this line, the chances are high that he or she will also possess a line of intuition.

Line of Intuition

The line of intuition is a fine line that runs from the base of the palm on the little finger side towards the center of the palm. It is usually a short, fine line, though you'll sometimes find people with long lines of intuition. These long lines are helpful, as they provide clues as to how the person will use his or her psychic abilities. If the line heads towards the head line, the person will have a talent at psychic or spiritual healing. If the line heads towards the destiny line, the person's psychic talents will be in the area of telepathy, clairvoyance, or precognition. This doesn't necessarily mean a person can't be both a healer and a clairvoyant; it's possible, but this person's innate talents will be revealed by the direction the intuition line heads towards.

Every now and again you'll meet someone who has two parallel intuition lines. This person will receive premonitions in his or her dreams.

People with intuition lines are caring, sensitive, sympathetic, and intuitive.

The Ring of Saturn

The ring of Saturn is a fine semi-circular line beneath the Saturn (second) finger. It is usually a single line, but is sometimes composed of two or three overlapping lines. The ring of Saturn is a negative line as someone who possesses it always expects to fail. This person will be full of self-doubt, low self-esteem, and negative thoughts. Naturally, this makes it considerably difficult for the person to succeed at anything. Whenever you see the ring of Saturn, you should gently encourage the person to set some goals and persist until he or she has achieved them.

I have seen instances where this line appeared after a major tragedy and then disappeared again once the person starting moving forwards again.

Via Lasciva

The Via Lasciva is usually a straight line that starts from the mount of Luna and heads partway towards the thumb. Sometimes this line is slightly curved.

In the past, this line had a bad reputation, and people with it were said to overindulge in sex and drugs. The word "lascivious" comes from the Latin *lasciva*. Even today, some palmistry books still repeat these myths from the past. People with a Via Lasciva on their palms are more easily affected by alcohol and drugs than most people. Naturally, once they've overindulged, their inhibitions are loosened. This is probably how this line gained its name and reputation.

Nowadays, the presence of this line shows the person always needs something exciting to look forward to. This often results in an adventurous and exciting life, as someone with this line will pursue activities that people without it might think twice about.

Loyalty Line

The loyalty line is common, and shows loyalty to home, family and the various organizations the person might belong to. The loyalty line runs from the base of the thumb to the life line. It is noticeably stronger than the fine worry lines that are frequently found in this position.

Mars Line

The Mars line is a short line found on the inner mount of Mars, inside the life line. It parallels the start of the life line. This line shows the person has an excellent metabolism, and is likely to be interested in sports and other physical activities.

Relationship Lines

Relationship lines are found on the side of the hand between the heart line and the base of the Mercury (little) finger. These lines are often called marriage lines, but this is incorrect as these relationships do not necessarily indicate marriages. Relationship lines indicate the number of important relationships a person will have. Most people have between one and four of these lines, and they are read from the heart line down to the little finger. For a relationship to become permanent, the line needs to come up the side of the palm and on to the palm itself. If a relationship is strong, but then ends and later starts again, it will be indicated by two lines, even though it is with the same person.

Relationship lines indicate the person's potential rather than the actuality. Consequently, if someone is extremely happy in his or her first marriage but has two more lines ahead, it doesn't mean that the current relationship will necessarily end.

To complicate matters still further, I have seen a relationship line appear on the hands of a woman shortly after she met the man she later married. Consequently, these lines can and do change. I've also met a few married men who had no relationship lines on their hands. This showed that the marriage was comfortable and convenient, but was not of major importance to them.

Children Lines

Children lines reflect a woman's potential, rather than the actuality. Nowadays, people can control how many children they have, but a century ago women often gave birth to their full potential.

The children lines are fine vertical lines under the Mercury finger. Lines indicating boys are longer and wider than lines indicating girls. A forked line indicates twins. As these lines are fine and hard to see, you might need a magnifying glass to find them. The stronger lines are said to indicate the number of children the person will have, but this is complicated as these lines actually indicate all the children the person is close to. Consequently, nieces, nephews, and the children of close friends might also be indicated.

Theoretically at least, a man has unlimited potential. Consequently, a man's hand indicates the number of children he is close to. Sooner or later, you'll meet a man who has, say, three children, but only two are indicated on his hand. This doesn't mean that he's not the father of the third child. It simply means that he is close to two of his children, but may not have a close relationship with the third.

A man I knew had a child when he was very young. The relationship did not last, and he lost contact with his son soon after he was born. He later married and had three more children. These children showed up as three strong lines on his hand, showing he was close to them. Many years later, he regained contact with his first child, who was now an adult. They quickly bonded, and in a matter of months, the man's hand showed four children lines.

New children lines can appear quickly. A friend of mine had no children lines on her hand and had given up hope of ever having children. She finally managed to adopt a baby, and in less than three months she also gained a proud children's line.

The Teacher's Square

A small square directly under the first finger is known as the teacher's square. Someone with it has the ability to explain new concepts and ideas to others in a clear and effective way. This person would make a natural teacher. You'll find this square on the hands of the very best teachers, but most of the time you'll find them on the hands of people who are not involved in the teaching profession. These people would have made good teachers, but preferred to pursue another type of career. These people will still make use of their teacher's square whenever they are dealing with or explaining something to others. Many people with a teacher's square conduct classes, seminars, and workshops, or teach a hobby at some stage in their lives.

Medical Stigmata

The medical stigmata, or samaritan lines, are a series of three or four fine vertical lines below the Mercury (little) finger. They are sometimes slightly offset towards the Apollo (ring) finger.

People with the medical stigmata have a natural empathy for all living things. They have a strong inbuilt desire to help others. As they also possess a healing touch, these people frequently choose a career in one of the healing professions. Consequently, you'll find the medical stigmata on the hands of good doctors, nurses, naturopaths, physiotherapists, veterinarians, and anyone else involved in the healing arts. You'll also find this mark on many gardeners, especially the ones said to have green thumbs. These people heal and nurture plants as they work with them.

Indicators of Money

Once you start reading palms, you'll find many people asking you questions about money. Three types of money are shown on the hand: inherited money, earned money, and money won by chance.

Inherited money is indicated by a fine line on the little finger side of the Apollo (ring) finger. This line is at the base of the finger and curves partway around the finger. Unfortunately, this line is not very helpful. If it's present, the person will inherit money at some stage of his or her life. This line does not indicate when this will occur, or if it has already occurred. Neither does it indicate how much money is involved.

Earned money is shown by a triangle in the middle of the palm. Two sides of the triangle are formed by the crossing of the head and destiny lines. A third line on the little finger side of the destiny line completes the triangle. The triangle rests on the wrist side of the head line. Ideally, this triangle should be completely closed, as this enables the person to hang on to some of the money earned. If the triangle is partially open, money will come in, but most of it will escape again.

The larger the triangle, the greater the person's potential to earn money. However, you need to look at other parts of the hand to see if the person has the necessary creativity, ambition, and persistence to achieve it. Someone with a large triangle but no motivation will not make anywhere near the amount of money possible.

If the money triangle has a fine line inside it, parallel to the third line, the person will be a good saver, and ultimately be in a position to make investments.

Easy money such as a lottery or casino win is indicated by a small triangle on the thumb side of the life line. One of the three sides of the triangle is formed by the life line. This helps date when the lucky win will occur.

The size of the triangle gives some indication as to the size of the win. However, you need to gauge the person's total circumstances to gauge this accurately. If someone is already wealthy, and wins, say, $100,000, it may not show up in the palm, as this amount is not a large sum for this person. If a beggar living on the streets won $100,000, it would show up as a large triangle. The amount won needs to be a significant sum of money for the person concerned to show up on the hand.

Sadly, you will not find many of these easy money triangles, as most people have to earn their money.

The Mystic Cross

As a palmist, you'll find many people asking you if they have a mystic cross on their hands. I have no idea why so many people ask about this. I guess it's probably because the name "mystic cross" is exotic and people think it makes them special in some way. Mystic crosses are common, and you will see them frequently. The mystic cross consists of two short lines that cross each other. It is situated in the quadrangle, the space between the heart and head lines.

The mystic cross does not touch any other lines, not even the head or heart lines. In a sense, it's floating entirely on its own.

The mystic cross shows an interest in the psychic world, and someone with it usually has a strong intuitive sense. The person may find that hunches are generally correct and this helps in making the right decision more often than not as life progresses. If offered a job, for instance, someone with the mystic cross will instinctively know if it is a good idea to accept it. Someone with a mystic cross can also use intuition to help friends and family.

The Rascettes

The rascettes are the lines that encircle the wrist at the very base of the palm. They are often referred to as the "bracelets." Gypsy palmists say that each rascette indicates twenty-five years of life. However, this is not correct, as most people have three rascettes and don't suddenly die at the age of seventy-five.

Traditionally, the rascettes were considered a sign of good luck, and the more bracelets you had, the luckier you were supposed to be. Modern day palmists do not usually read the rascettes. However, scientists have confirmed something about them that palmists have known for thousands of years. If the top rascette arches upwards into the palm, it is a sign of gynecological problems and difficulties in childbirth. In Greek times, women with this formation on their hands became vestal virgins at temples and were not allowed to marry.

While looking at the minor lines on the palm, you may have noticed some of the different skin ridge patterns that appear on the surface of the skin. The study and interpretation of skin ridge patterns is called *dermatoglyphics*, and is the subject of the next chapter.

THE SKIN RIDGE
PATTERNS

DERMATOGLYPHICS IS THE STUDY OF the skin ridge patterns found on the hands and feet. Dr. Harold Cummins, professor of Microscopic Anatomy at the Tulane University of Medicine, created the word *dermatoglyphics* in 1926[1]. Fingerprints are the best-known examples of dermatoglyphics. Palmists examine the fingerprints and the other skin ridge patterns when giving a reading.

In 1858, Sir William Herschel, a chief magistrate in imperial India, asked a businessman to place his handprint on the back of a contract to prevent him from denying the contract at a later date. As this proved effective, Sir William continued with the practice and built up a large collection of handprints. Later he collected prints of the person's right index and second finger. Sir William gradually discovered that each print was different and could prove a person's identity.

Sir Francis Galton (1822–1911), the English scientist, explorer, and writer, developed the first workable system of fingerprint classification, which he included in his monumental work, *Finger Prints* (London: Macmillan and Company, 1892). This book conclusively demonstrated that everyone's fingerprints are different; even identical twins have different fingerprints. Lines on the palms can change as a person goes through life but fingerprints never change.

Fingerprint Patterns

Sir Francis Galton based his classification system on the three main fingerprint patterns: loops, whorls, and arches (figure 9A).

LOOPS

A loop looks like a teardrop lying on its side. They are by far the most common of the three fingerprint patterns. In fact, between sixty and sixty-five percent of the population has loops on every fingertip. People with loops on every finger are adaptable and easy to get along with. They are flexible and able to adjust to any kind of situation. They go with the flow, and prefer to avoid the limelight. People with loops on every finger need a reasonable amount of variety in their lives to be happy.

Someone with a loop on the Jupiter finger will be sociable, charming, thoughtful, caring, and versatile.

A loop on the Saturn finger indicates the person has no considered ideas of his or her own. This individual will

Figure 9A: Whorl, Loop, and Arch—Fingerprint Patterns

enjoy discussions on a wide range of topics, and will express the views of others in the group, rather than develop original opinions.

A loop on the Apollo finger enhances the person's appreciation of anything new or beautiful. This person will make the most of new experiences, and enjoy being the first in the group to have them.

A loop on the Mercury finger indicates someone who can learn anything that interests him or her without great effort. This person will also be able to express him- or herself diplomatically and tactfully.

A loop on the thumb enables the person to get his or her way most of the time. These people can be rigid and stubborn, yet still have the ability to persuade others to do what they want.

Loops come in three forms: ulnar, radial, and composite. Ulnar loops start on the Mercury finger side of the finger, and head towards the thumb. In other words, the loop is open on the Mercury finger side of the particular finger. These loops are named after the ulnar bone in the arm.

Radial loops start on the thumb side of the finger and head towards the Mercury finger. They are relatively uncommon and are named after the radial bone on the thumb side of the arm. When found, they are usually on the Jupiter finger. Someone with radial loops will feel insecure and be constantly frustrated by the needs of others.

Composite loops are extremely rare and appear as a combination of ulnar and radial loops in the one fingerprint pattern. Someone with a composite loop will be in favor of something one minute, and opposed to it the next. This person will also have constant ups and downs in his or her emotional state.

WHORLS

Whorls look like a series of concentric circles. Approximately thirty to thirty-five percent of people have a whorl. A whorl shows that the person is slightly different and marches to the beat of a different drummer. This person will be energetic, ambitious, independent, original, and creative. Whorl people will not like to be hurried into making a decision, and because of this may be accused of stubbornness. It is extremely unusual to find someone with a whorl on each finger. The presence of a whorl gives originality to the quality indicated by the finger. Someone with whorls on most fingertips will be highly individualistic and find it hard to fit in with others.

Someone with a whorl on the Jupiter finger will be ambitious and have a strong desire to make his or her mark on life. Because this person has an unorthodox approach, it usually takes considerable time to find the right opportunity to pursue. Whorls are found frequently on the Jupiter fingers of self-employed people.

Someone with a whorl on the Saturn finger will be analytical and enjoy detailed work. This person is likely to be fascinated by anything that is different or out of the ordinary and will not be easily swayed by others.

Someone with a whorl on the Apollo finger will be full of original and creative ideas that may shock or surprise others. A whorl on the Apollo finger is a great asset to an artist as it ensures his or her work is strikingly different and original. Whorls are found on the Apollo finger more frequently than any other finger.

Someone with a whorl on the Mercury finger will be a highly entertaining conversationalist with fresh and original ideas. He or she will be attracted by anything unusual or unorthodox. It is rare to find a whorl on the Mercury finger.

Someone with a whorl on the thumb will be ambitious, motivated, and highly persistent. He or she will also be stubborn and highly independent. Once a goal has been set, this person will not give up until he or she has achieved it. This person will always use his or her own distinct approach to tasks, regardless of what other people might think or say.

ARCHES

Arches look like a gently rolling hill or wave. Only about five percent of the population has arches. They belong to people who are practical, reliable, responsible, and conscientious.

They live in the real world. People with arches on every finger are honest and dependable. They are prepared to speak their minds when necessary.

Those with an arch on the Jupiter finger will work hard to achieve a position of responsibility and power. These people enjoy power for its own sake. These people will adopt a cautious and patient approach, and may suffer from lack of confidence early in life.

Those with an arch on the Saturn finger will be naturally reticent, and dislike talking about themselves. These people will have strong beliefs about honesty, justice, and fairness.

Those with an arch on the Apollo finger will enjoy expressing themselves through practical activities, such as arts and crafts.

Those with an arch on the Mercury finger will find it hard to express themselves verbally, and appear quiet and secretive as a result. It is difficult for these people to open up to others.

People with an arch on the thumb will be down-to-earth, capable, persistent, and sensible but will tend to distrust others.

Tented Arch

You will sometimes see a variation of the arch, known as a tented arch. This is a high arch that looks similar to the loop. It is well named, as it looks something like a tent with a pole in the center to hold it up. Someone with a tented arch will be naturally enthusiastic. This person will be excited by anything new, but these interests are usually short-lived. He or she will be impulsive and full of nervous energy. Many people with a tented arch are musical.

Those with a tented arch on the Jupiter finger will lead pleasant and successful lives. These people will have many friends and achieve success in career and vocations. It is rare to see a tented arch on the Jupiter finger.

Someone with a tented arch on the Saturn finger will have a serious approach to life. This person will be idealistic, and need much time alone escaping from the day-to-day problems of life.

A tented arch on the Apollo finger denotes an enthusiastic, impulsive, and emotional person. He or she will be full of ideas, most of which will be totally impractical. This person could be highly creative, but will need constant guidance from friends and loved ones to achieve any degree of success.

Those with a tented arch on the Mercury finger will be talented at speaking and writing. These people will have humanitarian ideals and will probably use these talents to help others. It's extremely rare to find a tented arch on the Mercury finger.

People with a tented arch on the thumb will get along with almost everyone. These people will be entertaining, diplomatic, and charming. Charm, humor, or gentle persuasion are usually how these people achieve their goals.

Tri-radii

The tri-radii are the small triangles formed by the skin ridge patterns that indicate the apex of the mounts below each finger (figure 9B). A tri-radius is also often found on the mount of Luna, and occasionally on the mount of Neptune. A tri-radius on the mount of Neptune shows significant psychic potential.

The tri-radii should be situated at the top of each mount. This enhances the potential of the mount. Usually, though, the apex is slightly displaced and appears on the slopes of the mount rather than on the top.

APEX OF JUPITER

The tri-radius on the mount of Jupiter should be situated at the top of the mount, and in line with the center of the Jupiter finger. This denotes someone who is honest, ethical, trustworthy, and open.

It is more likely that the tri-radius will be sited towards the Saturn finger. This puts a quieter, more practical slant on the interpretation of the mount.

If the tri-radius is sited close to the thumb side of the palm, the person will be impulsive and lack a sense of responsibility.

If the tri-radius is situated close to the base of the Jupiter finger, the person will have an intellectual approach to life. He may appear condescending and find it hard to relate well with others.

Figure 9B: Tri-Radius

If the tri-radius is centrally situated, but is well away from the base of the Jupiter finger, the person will have humanitarian ideals and enjoy helping others

APEX OF SATURN

If the tri-radius is centrally situated directly below the Saturn finger, the person will think matters through and will possess good judgment. He or she will be direct and become impatient with people who talk around an issue rather than discussing it openly.

If the tri-radius is displaced towards the Apollo finger, the person will be extravagant and have no concept of the value of money.

I have never seen a mount of Saturn tri-radius displaced towards the Jupiter finger. I am sure it has occurred, but if so, it is extremely rare.

If the tri-radius is centrally situated close to the base of the Saturn finger, the person will need space and room away from others. This person will be more interested in learning for learning's sake, rather than practical application.

A tri-radius that is centrally situated but well away from the base of the Saturn finger indicates an interest in property and real estate; these are excellent career choices for people with this mark on their hands.

APEX OF APOLLO

If the tri-radius is centrally situated in line with the center of the Apollo finger, the person will have good taste and a strong appreciation of beauty in all its forms. This person would do well in a creative field, either in its creating or dealing. All these characteristics are enhanced if the tri-radius is close to the base of the Apollo finger.

A tri-radius displaced towards the Saturn finger indicates frequent doubt of one's creative abilities. This is especially the case if the person's Apollo finger slants towards the Saturn finger.

If the tri-radius is displaced towards the Mercury finger, the person will be able to make a comfortable living from some form of creative endeavor. This may be work the person creates or possibly dealing in work created by others. These people will be shrewd and able to quickly assess the market value of their or others' work.

APEX OF MERCURY

If the tri-radius is centrally sited under the Mercury finger, the person will love both the written and spoken word. You will seldom find a tri-radius in this position.

It is more usual for the tri-radius to be displaced towards the Apollo finger. Unfortunately, although the love of words remains, the person's verbal skills lessen the closer the tri-radius is to the Apollo finger.

Loop Patterns

There are thirteen different loop patterns that can be found on the palm (figure 9C). Most people have one or two of these loops, but many people have none of them. You may need a magnifying glass to identify them initially. Once you've seen a few of them, you'll have no difficulty in locating them when they are present.

THE LOOP OF HUMOR

This is the most commonly found loop. It is located between the Mercury and Apollo fingers. It gives the person a slightly different, offbeat sense of humor. The larger the loop is, the greater the person's sense of the ridiculous. Someone with a small loop of humor will enjoy practical jokes. The absence of this loop does not mean the person is lacking in humor.

THE LOOP OF EGO

This loop is sometimes confused with the loop of humor as it also starts between the Mercury and Apollo fingers. However, the loop of ego always slants towards the mount of Apollo. As its name indicates, someone with a loop of ego

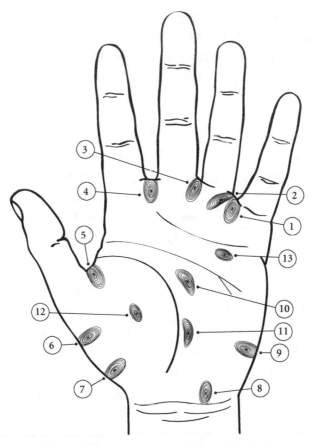

1. Loop of Humor
2. Loop of Ego
3. Loop of Common Sense
4. Rajah Loop
5. Loop of Courage
6. Loop of Response
7. Loop of Music

8. Loop of Inspiration
9. Ulnar Loop
10. Loop of Memory
11. Humanitarian Loop
12. Loop of Stringed Music
13. Loop of Recall

Figure 9C: Loops in the Palm

will have a strong sense of his or her self-importance, but he or she will be extremely sensitive, also. Consequently, he or she will possess a delicate, easily hurt ego.

THE LOOP OF COMMON SENSE

Situated between the Apollo and Saturn fingers, this loop denotes one who will think before acting and possession of a strong sense of responsibility. He or she will also enjoy helping others. Because of this, this loop is sometimes called the "loop of good intent." Not surprisingly, many members of service organizations and other community groups have a loop of common sense on their hands.

THE RAJAH LOOP

The rajah loop is comparatively rare. It is situated between the Saturn and Jupiter fingers. People with this loop are charismatic and possess a special aura that attracts people to them. They possess significant leadership qualities. This loop gained its name from Indian palmistry. In their system, people with it were believed to descend from royalty. People with this loop have a regal air around them, but I've no idea if everyone with it has royal ancestors!

THE LOOP OF COURAGE

The loop of courage is situated between the base of the thumb and the start of the life line on the inner mount of Mars. People with a loop of courage are brave, forceful, fearless, and prepared to stand up for their beliefs. They demonstrate moral as well as physical courage.

THE LOOP OF RESPONSE

The loop of response is situated on the edge of the mount of Venus, between the base of the thumb and the wrist. People with a loop of response instinctively respond to the feelings of the people they happen to be with at any time. If everyone is having fun, they'll have fun, too. If the group is serious or somber, they'll feel the same. This chameleon-like ability to fit in is entirely subconscious.

These people also respond to their environments in the same way. If their surroundings are dingy and dirty, they'll feel downhearted and depressed. If their environment is comfortable and pleasant, they'll feel positive and enthusiastic. Because they respond so quickly and markedly to their environment, they are likely to suffer mental problems if imprisoned or confined for any length of time.

People with the loop of response enjoy brass music, and frequently play a brass instrument. Even if they don't play an instrument, they'll enjoy attending a band concert.

THE LOOP OF MUSIC

The loop of music is situated on the outside of the mount of Venus close to the wrist. People with this loop have a great love for music. Even if they don't have a talent for composing or playing music, they'll thoroughly enjoy listening to good music.

THE LOOP OF INSPIRATION

The loop of inspiration is located on the mount of Neptune at the base of the palm. People with this loop are greatly moved, inspired, and motivated by anything that affects them at a deep level. This is usually music, literature, or humanitarian actions but can be anything these people find uplifting. This loop is extremely rare and those who possess it have the ability to inspire others and make the world a better place for everyone.

THE ULNAR LOOP

The ulnar loop is situated on the edge of the palm on the mount of Luna. This loop is sometimes called the loop of nature, as the people who have it enjoy a special relationship with the natural world. Conservationists, gardeners, and animal lovers are all likely to have an ulnar loop on their hands.

If the ulnar loop starts at least halfway along the mount of Luna towards the wrist, the person has unique access to his or her subconscious mind. This means the person is motivated more by the subconscious mind than the conscious mind. Not surprisingly, people with this loop have an unusual slant on life that makes them appear slightly "different."

The ulnar loop is most frequently found on the hands of people with Down's syndrome. In fact, ninety percent of them have this loop. It's interesting to reflect that many people with Down's syndrome have a great love of nature.

You will see this loop frequently, as it's also found on the hands of about eight percent of the general population.

THE LOOP OF MEMORY

The loop of memory is situated diagonally in the center of the palm, with one end indicating the mount of Jupiter, and the other the mount of Luna. It frequently runs parallel to the head line. As its name suggests, people with the loop of memory have extremely good memories. A close relative of mine has an incredible memory for facts, especially dates. If we happen to mention a family picnic we went on twenty or more years ago, he'll immediately be able to give us the day and date it occurred. He has the loop of memory on his hand.

THE HUMANITARIAN LOOP

The humanitarian loop is situated in the center of the palm, parallel to the destiny line. It is extremely rare. People with this loop are idealistic visionaries who find it hard to live in the real world. They experience more than their share of disillusionment and disappointment as they attempt to change the world and make it a better place for everyone.

THE LOOP OF STRINGED MUSIC

The loop of stringed music is situated on the center of the mount of Venus. It is extremely rare. This loop is similar to the loop of music, but the people who have it prefer music played by string instruments. Consequently, they'll probably prefer chamber music to a symphonic concert.

THE LOOP OF RECALL

The loop of recall is situated in the quadrangle, between the heart and head lines. People with it possess retentive memories and the ability to recall information whenever it is required. This ability is enhanced if the head line runs over this loop. If you find someone who has both the loop of memory and the loop of recall, he or she will have an excellent brain coupled with an almost photographic memory.

Dermatoglyphics is a comparatively new area of palmistry, and it's still possible for people to make new discoveries with it. Whenever possible, take palm prints of people who have interesting skin ridge patterns. You will find these useful for reference purposes, and ultimately you'll have your own personal library of every possible loop and tri-radius.

It's important to relate the skin ridge patterns to the rest of the hand, rather than interpreting them on their own. Often the skin ridge patterns will reinforce what you've already discovered about the person. However, you will find contradictions at times. This is as it should be, as we all have contradictory sides to our personalities. At one time I worked for a miserly boss who was always generous with beggars he passed on the street. I never had the opportunity to look at his palms, but was extremely aware of his large, stubborn thumbs.

OTHER MARKS
ON THE PALM

In addition to the lines, mounts, and skin ridge patterns, you will find a number of other markings on the hands, some of which can be used to add great detail to your readings. The most important markings are squares, crosses, triangles, and stars. You will sometimes see these on the major lines, but at other times they'll stand on their own, and the area of the palm they are sited in will give you a clue as to their purpose.

Squares

There are two types of squares: protective and restrictive. Protective squares enclose breaks in the lines. They are highly positive as they nurture and protect the person. Protective squares are most commonly found on the life line. In this position, they protect the person from a potentially serious illness. Protective squares on other lines provide the person with the necessary strength and energy to overcome whatever difficulty is indicated by the line. Squares are seldom perfectly square, and are often oblong in shape.

Restrictive squares do not cover breaks in the lines. They usually mean confinement. The most obvious example of this is imprisonment, but people who are trapped in difficult situations are also confined by circumstances, and the restrictive square will last until they manage to find a solution. A square on the mount of Venus that is not attached to the life line is a sign of emotional confinement. Someone who feels trapped in an unhappy relationship is likely to have one or more of these squares.

Crosses

In the past, crosses were considered a negative sign in palmistry. Nowadays, they are usually considered to indicate a time when the person pauses, takes stock of his or her situation, and then moves forward again. In effect, crosses indicate a crossroads in a person's life. He or she pauses before deciding which path to take. Many people are reluctant to make a change: crosses indicate when they'll be forced to make this change.

Crosses are useful because they frequently warn people of potential difficulties. Once someone is aware of a potential problem, he or she can take steps to avert it. A cross touching the life line, for instance, is a sign of potential home and family difficulties. A cross touching the destiny line warns of a potential accident. A cross that touches the health line indicates potential health problems.

A cross inside the quadrangle, created by the destiny line and a minor line, is a sign of success achieved after a long struggle. This cross is a positive one, as it denotes success, but it's also a frustrating factor as far as the person who has it is concerned.

A cross on the mount of Jupiter shows that the person is ready to change the direction of his or her life. This could be a new partner, but may also be related to spiritual growth, or confidence and self-esteem.

Crosses on the other mounts indicate problems that need to be resolved in the areas indicated by the mount.

Triangles

Triangles provide enthusiasm, impetus, and energy. They show the person has a quick brain, and can understand the essentials of a situation at a glance. It also means that the person has the potential to succeed in a scientific or creative career.

Triangles on a mount increase the positive qualities of the mount. A triangle on the mount of Venus shows that the person will marry for money, and that the marriage will be a happy and long-lasting one.

Stars

Stars are created when three or more minor lines cross each other. Stars are extremely positive indications of success when found on one of the mounts. This means the person has the opportunity to achieve great success in the area indicated by the mount. A star on the mount of Jupiter, for instance, shows that the person will be honored for his or her achievements.

Unfortunately, stars found elsewhere on the hand indicate that the person will become involved in situations that are out of his or her control. The placement of the star frequently indicates what area of life the difficulty will occur in.

Grilles

Grilles are formed when several minor lines crisscross each other to create a pattern that looks like a grill. They are normally found on the mounts, and show that the person tends to act too hastily. This is frustrating to everyone, including the person, who generally fails to see the situation as it really is.

If the grille is found on a flat or invisible mount, the person will be emotionally cold. The grille represses the good qualities of a normal sized mount, and tends to enhance the negative traits.

On the mount of Venus, a grille enhances the person's natural passion, but makes it hard for him or her to use it responsibly.

On the mount of Luna, it creates a scattered, unfocused imagination. Someone with a grille in this position will be hard to please.

On the mount of Jupiter, it makes the person overly proud and selfish.

On the mount of Saturn, it increases the person's Saturnine qualities, making him or her gloomy, untrusting, and secretive.

On the mount of Apollo, it gives the person a strong desire for fame and the rewards associated with it. Unfortunately, it also scatters this person's energies, making it even more difficult for this person to achieve goals.

A grille on the mount of Mercury shows dishonesty and a habit of stretching the truth.

Circles

Circles are seldom seen on a palm. Usually, this is fortunate, as circles are considered an indication that the person is weak and unable to stand up for him- or herself. However, there is one exception to this. A circle on the mount of Apollo indicates success and fame in a creative field.

Dots and Spots

Indented dots and spots on a major line reveal a blockage of energy. When found on the life line, a dot or spot indicates a physical illness. On the head line, a dot or spot indicates stress, negativity, and the possibility of a breakdown.

On the destiny line, a dot or spot indicates a time when the person pauses and reevaluates his or her career. A dot on the heart line indicates emotional problems. However, a white dot on the heart line is a sign of a good relationship that begins after the person has recovered from serious difficulties.

Islands

Islands appear on the lines of the hand, and are never found on their own. An island indicates a weakness in the line, and this reduces the amount of energy the person has available to handle anything that is occurring in his or her life relating to the line at the time indicated by the placement of the island.

Chains

Chains are a series of islands that are linked together, forming a chain. One island indicates a weakness; a series of islands indicates a lengthy period of weakness, indecision, and lack of energy. Naturally, this causes major problems in the area of life indicated by the particular line the chain is on. Chains are commonly found on the heart line, denoting a period in which expressing emotions is difficult.

———————

As with the skin ridge patterns, these markings should not be interpreted on their own. They are useful because they provide extra information that confirms or denies other information that you've found on the palm.

In the next two chapters, we'll incorporate everything we've covered so far to prepare you for the numerous questions you'll receive about love and career. We'll start with arguably the most important topic of all: love and romance.

11

.....

LOVE AND
ROMANCE

MANY PEOPLE COME FOR A palm reading because they want to learn more about their love life. As a palmist, you're likely to receive more questions about this aspect of life than any other. This isn't surprising, as everyone wants to love and be loved. Even people in happy relationships will want assurance that it's going to last.

People come together for a variety of reasons. Someone who is lonely might want a partner purely for company. Another person might seek a partner who can provide a trait that he or she is missing. Someone else might want to be in a relationship for regular sex, financial security, or respectability. Most people want to be in a deep, close, loving relationship that builds and grows with time. Sadly, divorce statistics show that many relationships fail to last. As a palmist, you'll be able to counsel, guide, and advise people in the areas of love and relationships by recognizing their underlying motivations and helping them realize their strengths and weaknesses.

You can determine how romantic someone is by examining the mount of Venus. A high, reasonably firm mount of Venus reveals someone who is romantic, passionate, and full of energy. This person would be happiest in a relationship with someone who had a similarly shaped mount of Venus.

A person's heart line will give you clues about his or her emotional life. Islands, chains, and breaks in this line all affect the person's emotional life and the ability to give and receive love.

Someone with a head line that curves towards the mount of Luna will be able to express his or her romantic feelings more easily than someone with a head line that is straight. However, if the head line ends well inside the mount of Luna, the person will live in a world of romantic fantasies, and is likely to be disappointed and disillusioned with the reality.

It is also a good idea to look for relationship lines, children lines, Girdle of Venus, and the loop of humor. These also affect the person's love life. Someone who is lacking any relationship lines, for instance, may desire a partner for self-gratification, rather than a desire to love and be loved. However, you must always remember that lines can appear. If this person happened to meet the right person for him or her, and fell in love, a relationship line would appear in a matter of months.

Children lines show that the person likes children. The presence of these lines does not necessarily indicate that the children are the sons and daughters of the person whose hand they appear on. This person might be a dedicated aunt or uncle, for instance. However, someone of childbearing age who has children lines on his or her hand should seek a partner who also has children lines.

Someone with a Girdle of Venus feels his or her emotions deeply, and needs a partner who respects this, and can express his or her feelings.

Every relationship has its share of ups and downs, and the presence of a loop of humor shows the person will be able to take these in his or her stride.

Compatability

As a palmist, you'll have the opportunity to read the hands of many couples. I enjoy this aspect of palmistry, especially if the couple is compatible. There are five main things to look for:

- The shape of the hand
- The heart line
- The thumb
- The mount of Venus
- The relationship lines

Hand Shapes

The hand shapes of the two people need to be looked at, as this reveals their basic temperaments. It is a positive sign for both people to have the same type of hand. For instance, air and air go well together, as they both have similar temperaments. This goes against the popular romantic idea that opposites attract. Opposites certainly do attract, but the interest may not last, as the major differences in outlook become more apparent. Long-term relationships are generally easier if both people think along the same lines. The best relationships occur when the two people have noticeable differences, as well as marked similarities.

Compatibility becomes slightly more complicated if the two people have different hand shapes. Fire and air get on well, as air stimulates fire. Air and earth get on well, too, as air enables living things to flourish on earth. Earth and water also get on well, as water enables life to live on earth. Fire and water do not get on well, as water puts out fire. Fire and earth do not get on, either, as fire scorches earth. Air and water do little for each other, making this an unexciting combination.

Heart Lines

The two major types of heart line—physical and mental—reveal how people approach matters of the heart. Someone with a physical heart line will be active in seeking and wooing a prospective partner. Conversely, someone with a mental heart line will need time to initiate a relationship.

The person with a physical heart line will actively search for a relationship while his or her mental heart line friend will be waiting for a relationship to occur. In addition, people with the two types of heart line express their feelings in different ways. Someone with a physical heart line will be demonstrative and find it easy to express feelings. Someone with a mental heart line will express feelings by being considerate and thoughtful. It may not occur to this person to express his or her feelings in words.

The ending position of the heart lines is important in determining compatibility. Ideally, the heart lines should end at the same place. If they end between the Jupiter and Saturn fingers, both partners will have realistic expectations about the relationship. If they end under the Jupiter finger, they will both be overly idealistic, and this can lead to disappointment. If they both end under the Saturn finger, they will be more concerned with their own needs, rather than those of their partner.

The situation becomes harder to read if one partner has a physical heart line and the other a mental heart line. The heart lines should still end under or between the same fingers. However, this couple will experience problems as the partner with a physical heart line will be able to express his or her innermost feelings more easily than his or her mental heart line partner. The partner with a mental heart line will need constant reassurance that he or she is loved.

You need to look at the rest of each person's heart line also, as this reveals the past romantic history. Most people have chained heart lines revealing previous disappointments in love. This sometimes makes it hard for them to trust others again. If one person has a clear heart line, he or she will need to be patient with a proposed partner who has a heavily chained heart line.

The Thumb

From a compatibility point of view, it's a good sign if both people have similar thumbs. If both have flexible thumbs, they'll get along extremely well, as they're willing to adapt and fit in. Two stubborn thumbs also work well, once they've learned to compromise. However, problems can arise if one person has a stubborn thumb and the other a small, flexible one. The person with the stubborn thumb will tend to dominate and bully his or her partner.

Problems can also arise if one person has a long thumb, and his or her partner has a short thumb. The person with a long thumb will be ambitious, while the other person will want a quiet home life with as little stress as possible.

Mount of Venus

Both partners should have mounts of Venus that are of similar height and firmness. This means they have similar levels of passion. Problems are likely to occur when one partner has a high, firm mount of Venus (giving a strong desire for sex), and the other a low mount (little interest in the subject).

Relationship Lines

The relationship lines on the side of the hand between the Mercury finger and the start of the heart line reveal how committed each person is to the relationship. These lines can be difficult to interpret, as previous important relationships need to be taken into account.

Once you have determined which line indicates the current relationship, examine it for both length and quality. A long, strong line is a positive indication, as it shows the person is prepared to commit him- or herself to the relationship. However, keep in mind that if the relationship is new, and the person has only one or two relationship lines, the line representing the new relationship may not have formed yet.

It is a good idea also to look at the relationship line preceding the one that represents the current relationship. If this line appears malformed, or has an island or spots on it, the person will still be harboring angry feelings about his or her former partner. The person will have to let go of these before committing fully to the new relationship.

Every now and again you'll meet people that are totally incompatible yet stay together, sometimes for decades. I knew a couple that argued constantly yet remained married for more than forty years. Another couple I knew lived in the same house and slept in the same bed, but did not speak to each other for the final twenty years of their relationship.

There is nothing you can do for these people as, in a strange sort of way, they seem to enjoy being miserable.

However, you'll also sometimes find couples with incompatible hands that make it work. I've learned that almost any combination can work if both partners love each other and work hard on their relationship. I've seen many relationships that, from a palmistry point of view, seemed totally incompatible, but yet managed to succeed, sometimes extremely well. I've also seen other couples who seemed perfect from a compatibility point of view, but were unable to make the relationship last. As a palmist, you can advise and guide, but ultimately it is up to people themselves.

12
.....

CHOOSING
A CAREER

Palmists receive more questions about love and romance than any other subject. However, questions about work and career follow closely behind. These vary from teenagers anxious to find out what type of work they would be best suited for, to middle-aged people who are seeking a change of career; even people seeking part-time work in their retirement are curious. Nowadays, many people have been made redundant from their jobs and seek help on finding work they would find satisfying and enjoyable.

In the past, people would seek a secure job and continue in that field until they retired. Today, the fast-paced world we live in sees many people changing careers regularly.

All this means that people of any age will ask you questions about their careers.

The first thing to look at from a vocational analysis point of view is the shape of the hands.

Earth Hands
(Square Palm, Short Fingers)

People with earth hands are reliable, dependable, cautious, practical, and hard-working. They enjoy routine, repetition, and order. Most of the time, they like to finish what they start. People with earth hands enjoy being outdoors, and are often found in practical type occupations such as building, farming, craftwork, and working with animals. People living in rural communities frequently have earth hands and it is this trait that gives them their strong affinity with nature. People with earth hands usually prefer working for others, but some become successful running their own businesses.

Air Hands
(Square Palm, Long Fingers)

People with air hands enjoy work that is mentally challenging. They like to finish what they start. People with air hands enjoy communication and are often found in the fields of television, radio, and public relations. They make successful teachers, salespeople, interviewers, and entertainers. Air-handed people are curious about virtually everything, and this makes them good researchers and writers.

Fire Hands
(Oblong Palm, Short Fingers)

People with fire hands are enthusiastic self-starters. They thrive on stress and work well with deadlines. In fact, without them, they'd find it hard to finish most of the activities they enter into with such enormous enthusiasm. They make good entrepreneurs but are better with "the big picture" than they are with details. People with fire hands enjoy occupations that provide plenty of change and variety.

Water Hands
(Oblong Palm, Long Fingers)

People with water hands are sympathetic and understanding. Consequently, they are often found in humanitarian type occupations such as nursing, teaching, social work, and childcare. People with water hands are also refined and have a strong aesthetic sense. Consequently, they frequently gravitate towards careers involving items they find to be attractive, such as clothing or jewelry.

Occupational Clues

There are a number of signs on the hands that provide clues as to the type of work someone would be interested in.

TEACHER'S SQUARE

The teacher's square is found beneath the Jupiter finger. People with a teacher's square have a talent for explaining things to others and therefore make excellent teachers or instructors. This teaching is often done outside an academic environment. Someone who has a talent for teaching others how to swim, drive a car, or construct a bookcase is likely to have a teacher's square on his or her palm. Sooner or later, someone with a teacher's square will find him- or herself imparting knowledge to others, and experiencing enormous joy and satisfaction as a result.

MEDICAL STIGMATA

The medical stigmata is a small group of vertical lines beneath the Mercury finger. People with it enjoy helping others, and frequently gravitate to the healing professions, such as medicine or veterinarian practice. They are also found on the hands of people involved in social work. Good gardeners sometimes possess a medical stigmata.

ANGLE OF PRACTICALITY

The Angle of Practicality is a distinct bump on the outside of the palm at the base of the second phalange of the thumb. People with this angle are good with their hands and enjoy using them to solve problems. Engineers, plumbers, electricians, and carpenters are examples of people likely to have an Angle of Practicality on their hands.

SQUARE FINGERTIPS

People with square fingertips are orderly, efficient, and accurate. They are often found in banking, finance, and accountancy positions. They also gravitate towards working in local government. People in banking and finance frequently have short middle phalanges on each finger.

THE MOUNTS

A firm and prominent or well-developed mount provides clues that can be used for vocational analysis. They reveal the person's talents, and indicate what he or she enjoys doing. Often, the mounts can be used to help people determine the right career.

The Jupiter mount gives leadership qualities. If this were the dominant mount on the hand, the person would be ambitious and will ultimately end up in a position of responsibility.

The Saturn mount is the least likely mount to be dominant in a hand. Someone with a prominent Saturn mount will be interested in science and could pursue a career as a researcher in a scientific field.

The Apollo mount gives the person a creative talent. This person would work well in some area of the arts.

The Mercury mount gives the person a talent at communication and business. This person would progress in a business environment using his or her significant communication skills.

The inner mount of Mars gives the person a talent at medicine, though other factors in the palm, such as the presence of a medical stigmata, need to be examined to see if this talent will develop. A strong inner mount of Mars is also useful to anyone involved in sales.

The outer mount of Mars gives the person a talent at competitive sports. People with a strong outer mount of Mars often take up careers in law enforcement, the armed forces, or security.

The mount of Luna gives the person a rich imagination. This talent can manifest itself in a variety of ways, such as writing, acting, and other creative activities.

The mount of Venus gives the person tremendous reserves of energy and a strong passion for life. This can be used in almost any career.

Talents

I believe everyone has a talent of some sort. When I mention talents, most people think of some form of creativity, but this is not necessarily the case. I know a waiter who has an incredible memory for names. If you have been to his restaurant at some time in the past, he will greet you by name when you return, no matter how many years later that might be. This is an incredible talent and it's been worth a fortune to him, as people love to be remembered. One of the most successful real estate agents I have ever met is a woman who instinctively knows which house is right for different people.

As a palmist, you'll meet many extremely talented people. You'll also find that most of these people do little to nothing with their talents. Sometimes the talent is unrecognized. Lack of motivation seems to be the main reason people don't develop their natural talents.

Of course, developing a talent usually involves considerable sacrifice. If you want to be a concert violinist, you'll have to practice for several hours a day, for years and years, in the hope of becoming successful. Many people are not prepared to pay that price.

Creative talents are clearly shown on the person's palms. A strong mount of Luna shows a creative imagination. A head line that heads towards Luna reveals a creative thinker. A strong mount of Apollo coupled with long first and second phalanges on the Apollo finger indicates artistic ability. The first phalange denotes ability, and the second phalange indicates good color sense. A talent for writing is shown by a good-length Mercury finger with a prominent second phalange. A head line that heads towards the mount of Luna indicates a creative writer who will probably write fiction. A straight head line indicates a writer who will prefer dealing with facts. A strong mount of Venus is also useful for creative writers. Not surprisingly, the presence of a writer's fork is a good sign for would-be writers.

Musical talents come out in many ways. The Angles of Practicality and Pitch, and strong Venus and Luna mounts accentuate musical gifts. Singing ability is often revealed by perfectly round fingers. Talented musicians are also likely to possess a loop of music, a loop of response, or the loop of stringed music.

TALENT IN BUSINESS

You will find self-employed people with every possible type of hand. A plumber, for instance, is likely to have a totally different hand than a salesperson or an accountant. However, there will also be some common points. Self-employed people usually have a strong thumb, as this gives them the necessary motivation and desire to succeed.

Most business people have a strong destiny line, as this gives a sense of direction. However, I have met a few successful business people who lack a destiny line. These people were fortunate enough to find something by chance that led them on to success.

A long, straight Mercury finger provides communication skills and a sense of shrewdness in financial dealings.

The Jupiter finger reveals how ambitious the businessperson is. Some people in business seek to make a fortune, while others are content with a business that provides little more than wages.

Ambition

Ambition is an essential requirement for worldly success. As a palmist, you will read the hands of many people who are talented in various ways, but do nothing with their innate talents because they lack this trait.

Ambition is revealed in a number of ways on the palm. The most important indicators are the length of the Jupiter finger and thumb, and a well-formed line of destiny. The head line and Mercury fingers also need to be examined.

A long Jupiter finger gives the person drive and leadership ability. A long thumb provides motivation for success. There are bound to be setbacks from time to time, and the person needs to be resilient enough to recover from these and keep on working towards his or her goal. A well-marked destiny line ensures that the person will be sufficiently persistent to keep on going until he or she achieves success.

The person's head line reveals how he or she thinks, and clearly shows if he or she has the necessary imagination to visualize success before working to achieve it. A good-length Mercury finger is also useful, as someone who is aiming to be successful needs the ability to communicate well with others.

HOW TO TAKE HAND PRINTS

WHENEVER POSSIBLE, TAKE PALM PRINTS of the people you read for. This serves a number of purposes. As you build up a collection of palm prints, you'll realize just how diverse people's hands are. You'll discover, for instance, that most people with earth hands have few lines on their palms, while people with water hands usually have many. It is often hard to see the fingerprints and dermatoglyphics on a palm, but they show up clearly on a palm print, making them much easier to read and interpret. I also enjoy collecting prints from different generations of the same family: it enables me to see from where different family traits and talents have come.

By taking palm prints, you'll see how people's hands change over time. It can be fascinating to see how someone's hands have progressed (or sometimes regressed) since you last looked at them. You'll also find it revealing to take prints of your own palms once a year, and see how your lines are changing to reflect what is going on in your life.

You might be fortunate enough to have a young child in your home. If you take a palm print of him or her every year, you'll be able to observe how the lines change and develop as he or she grows into adulthood.

When I was living in London as a young man, I was shown a huge collection of palm prints by the widow of a well-known palmist. The prints were delicate because they smudged easily. They were produced by a time-consuming process using candle black. A sheet of white paper was moved back and forth over a candle flame until the candle smoke covered the paper with black soot. The person's palms were then pressed on to this surface to take a print. The quality of print was excellent, but had to be handled extremely carefully. Fortunately, we no longer need to make prints this way.

Taking a Print

You'll need a supply of good quality bond paper that is at least eight and a half by eleven inches in size. You also need an ink roller, three to four inches wide, and a tube of artist's water-based black ink. You can obtain both of these at an art supply store.

In addition, you'll need a slightly spongy surface to put the paper on. At one time I used a large oblong of foam rubber, but found that a one-inch stack of folded tea towels worked better. It doesn't matter what you use, as long as it is flexible enough to take a print of the hollow of the palm.

Start by placing a sheet of paper on top of your stack of tea towels. Squeeze a small amount of ink onto a square of glass, or a spare piece of paper. Roll it with the roller until it is smooth, and the roller is covered with a fine, even surface of ink.

Ask the person you are reading for to remove any rings if they can, and then hold both hands out, palms upwards. Using long, even strokes of the roller, cover the palms with a fine coating of ink.

Tell the person to hold both hands naturally and to place them simultaneously on the sheet of paper. Once they have done this, press down gently on the back of each hand to ensure the center of the palm makes an impression on the paper. Hold down the ends of the paper and ask your client to raise both hands straight up in the air. Once he or she has done this, take separate prints of the thumb, as the hand print captures only the sides of the thumbs. Usually, I take two sets of palm prints, as this enables my client to take one set away with them.

It takes practice to get perfect palm prints every time. It can be difficult, for instance, to take a complete impression of the hands of people with high mounts of Venus and/or Luna. In these instances, I ask the client to raise both hands while still attached to the paper. I then gently press the paper into the hollow of their palms.

With practice, you'll take perfect prints almost every time. Many palmists prefer to take prints of the palms one at a time. I prefer to have both palms on the same sheet of paper, but it is definitely easier to do them separately.

As long as you use water-based ink, your clients will be able to remove the ink by washing their hands with soap and water. I start examining the prints while they are doing this.

Nowadays, digital cameras are one of the best ways to record people hands. You can take photographs of the front and back of each hand, and if you have a good quality camera, you can enlarge them to see every detail of the finest skin ridge patterns.

It's worth remembering that lipstick makes excellent prints if you happen to be out and about and have no other way to record the palms.

Photocopying machines also record the lines and skin ridge patterns well, but unfortunately the shape of the hand can change slightly as the person presses his or her palms on to the glass. Cover the person's hands with a white towel after they've been placed on the glass. This provides a white background. This makes the prints look more attractive, and also provides room for making notes.

Remember to date and identify the print. Some palmists write their notes beside the prints. I prefer to use a different sheet of paper for this, as I may not want the client to see my notes. On this sheet I also record other details that are not revealed in the prints, such as the flexibility of the hand, and the texture of the skin. I also make a note of anything else that seems relevant, such as the person's age, marital status, number of children he or she has, occupation, and important hobbies or interests.

Over time, you'll build up a valuable collection of palm prints that will become increasingly useful to you as you continue your study and research into this fascinating field.

14

.....

PUTTING IT ALL TOGETHER

You now know enough to give a full palm reading. Look at as many palms as possible. Give everyone a quick reading. As you learn more and gain confidence in your skills, you'll be able to give longer readings. Ask questions about anything unusual you see in someone's hands.

Get into the habit of reading palms in a set order. This ensures you cover everything, and don't accidentally leave anything out. I start by looking at both hands together. I then examine the dominant hand, determining its shape, firmness, and flexibility. I repeat this process with the other hand. I then return to the dominant hand to see if any mounts are more obvious than others. I repeat this with the other hand. After that, I return to the dominant hand and check the heart, head, and life lines, in that order. I'll also include any fine lines that relate to these lines, such as the Girdle of Venus or a sister line. I then examine the destiny line, followed by the thumb and fingers.

I'll follow this by examining the mounts, the minor lines, and the dermatoglyphics. I then repeat the process, in the same order, with the minor hand.

As I'm doing this, I check other aspects of the hand to see if they confirm anything I've just noticed. For instance, if I saw a writer's fork on the head line, I'd immediately look at the second phalange of the Mercury finger to see if the person was interested in creative writing, or if the writer's fork was being used to come up with practical ideas.

Here is the palm print of the right hand of a forty-four-year-old right-handed woman I'll call Monica (figure 14A). Before reading any further, see what you can ascertain from her palm.

Here is what I might say to her:

"You have a strong hand. It's firm and rigid, so you can stand up for yourself when necessary. You have what is known as an air hand, because you have a square-shaped palm with long fingers. This means you're a planner, a communicator, and, in some ways, a teacher. You have an extremely active mind. Whatever work you do at any stage needs to be mentally stimulating, and have plenty of variety. The only real disadvantage of all of this is that you invariably try to use logic in preference to your emotions.

"This is shown in your heart line, too. This line represents your emotional life. There have been a number of emotional ups and downs, some of them caused by your distrust or reluctance to allow your emotions full play. Fortunately, your heart line ends in the perfect place between your first and second fingers. The trident on the end shows

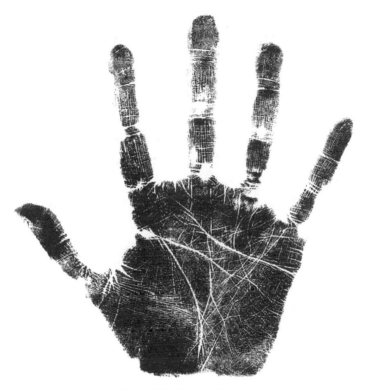

Figure 14A: Sample Print A

you have plenty of emotional energy, but might find it hard to make good use of it. Long term, it's a good sign, as it denotes a fortunate life. You have traces of what's known as a Girdle of Venus. This means you feel things deeply, and in the past, may have been hurt easily by the words and actions of others. That is much more under control now.

"You have a good practical brain, Monica. You're a logical thinker, and you like to compare and evaluate different choices before making up your mind. You keep your feet firmly on the ground, refusing to get carried away with dreams and fantasies. The writer's fork on your head line shows that you have the ability to come up with good ideas, and then turn around and make them practical.

"You're cautious, and like to think things through before moving forwards.

"Your life line is strong, clear and well-marked. You have strong reserves of energy and stamina. You have what is called a sister line. This protects your life line and gives you a good hold on life.

"You have your share of worry lines, these fine lines radiating out towards your life line. You worry when there's cause to worry, and there's no sign that they'll ever affect your health.

"Your destiny line is strong, too, but has a couple of major changes of direction on it. These are likely to be changes in the way you look at things, rather than major changes of career. Your destiny line continues well after crossing your heart line, so there'll be new and exciting opportunities for you in your fifties, sixties, and beyond.

"You have a strong thumb. It is a good length and is reasonably firm. This shows you can stand up for yourself. You need challenges, and do not give up easily. You have approximately the same amount of logic as willpower. This shows you can come up with a good idea, and then carry it through to completion.

"Your fingers are well balanced. Your little finger is set noticeably lower than the other fingers. This means you have to learn through experience. You'll make a number of mistakes as you go through life but will learn from all of them. Some of these mistakes almost certainly will be in the area of relationships. As your little finger is set well away from the others, you'll be an independent thinker, preferring to make up your own mind on different matters, rather than accepting other people's ideas without thinking them through.

"In palmistry, we're always looking for balance. Your index and ring fingers are approximately equal in length, Monica. This gives you the necessary drive, energy, and persistence to achieve your goals. The middle section (second phalange) of this finger is long. This gives you good taste. You work best in a pleasant environment. The fingerprint pattern on this finger is a whorl. This enhances your creativity, and gives originality to anything you produce.

"Your second finger is strong and straight. This shows you are responsible and use your common sense. The middle section is again longer than the others. This shows attention to detail.

"Your first finger is well balanced. The loop on the fingertip shows you're open and friendly. You probably get along well with virtually everyone. The base section of your thumb is strong. This means that at some time in your life you'll develop an interest in philosophy or spiritual matters. This may or may not be a church type religion. In fact, as you also have a good intuition line, it's likely to be a faith you build on your own.

"You have a teacher's square below your first finger. This shows that you can explain things clearly to others. It's found on the hands of the very best teachers, but most people who have one use it in everyday life, rather than in a classroom.

"You have a number of restlessness lines on the side of your hand. They used to be called travel lines, and they show you will travel at times. You enjoy planning the trips almost as much as taking them.

"Your health line is strong and clear. You pay attention to physical fitness, and this certainly pays off for you long term.

"You have three relationship lines. These show a potential, rather than the actuality. The third line is by far the strongest, and indicates a strong, ongoing relationship.

"Your money sign is a perfect triangle. It's a good size, and, because of your ability to plan ahead and work hard, you'll ultimately find yourself in a comfortable position financially.

"The cross in the quadrangle shows that everything takes time and effort. It makes you more of a plodder than a whiz kid. However, your pace gives you the necessary determination and persistence to ultimately succeed.

"You have a good sense of humor, a sense of the ridiculous. It's good that you have this, as it looks as if you frequently take life far too seriously. It does you good to laugh.

"You have a strong, capable hand, and you gain great satisfaction from setting and achieving your goals."

———————————

These hands belong to a successful businesswoman. Monica started her own cosmetics company when she was in her early thirties, and now exports her products around the world. This was her third attempt at starting a business. She has never married and now regrets focusing all her energies on her career. Her past relationships failed, she told me, because she found it hard to express her innermost feelings. She was extremely reserved the whole time she was with me. Most palm readings become conversations, and sometimes the client says more than the palm reader. That wasn't the case with this reading, as Monica said hardly anything while I was looking at her hands. Monica finds it hard to confide in anyone, and instead of discussing her concerns with others, releases them with regular workouts at the gym. This is good for her physical fitness, but she finds it frustrating that she can't discuss her private concerns with friends and family.

Most readings focus on a specific area of the person's life. The client might be concerned about love, health, or career, for instance. Monica gave me no clues as to what area she wanted me to concentrate on, and afterwards told me she had the reading solely out of curiosity. This is relatively unusual, as most people come for a private reading when they need help or advice.

Full-length readings involve looking at both hands, and I did this with Monica. This enabled me to make comparisons between her thoughts (non-dominant hand) and actions (dominant hand).

Here is another palm print for you to examine (figure 14B). This print belongs to a professional astrologer who is forty years old. He started his working life as a carpenter, and became fascinated with astrology in his early twenties. Although it's not really visible on the print, he has a good Angle of Practicality. This, plus the shape of his palm, shows that he is a practical person who is good with his hands. Consequently, when he left school with no idea as to what he wanted to do with his life, carpentry probably seemed like a good career choice.

Looking at the palm print, can you tell approximately how old he was when he discovered astrology? (Clue: look at his destiny line.)

What indications are there in his palm that reveal his interest in the metaphysical worlds? (Clue: look at the skin ridge patterns in his mount of Luna, and the Apollo and Mercury fingers, and his line of intuition.)

Is he an independent thinker? (Clue: head line, and Mercury finger set apart from the other fingers.)

Figure 14B: Sample Print B

Can you see any indications in his palm that indicate that he enjoys helping others? (Clue: loop of common sense. He also has a teacher's square, which is barely visible on the print.)

Would he be good at writing on astrology? (Clue: second phalange, and setting, of the Mercury finger.)

Did he lack confidence when he was younger? (Clue: Jupiter finger.)

Has he, or will he, make any money? (Clue: can you see a triangle made partially from his head and destiny lines?)

Has he had problems with close relationships in the past? (Clue: first part of his heart line.)

Does he keep good health? (Clue: life line and hepatica.)

Are you surprised he became a fulltime astrologer, or, after looking at his palm print, do you feel it was inevitable that he decided to make a career in a psychic field?

15
.....

CONCLUSION

I HAVE TRIED TO INCLUDE everything you need to know to read palms successfully in this book. Palmistry is a fascinating subject that has enthralled people for thousands of years. As your palmistry skills develop, you'll become more and more popular as people learn about your talent.

Although people might say they're having their palms read purely for fun, deep down they'll be concerned about what you might find in their hands. You must be gentle and kind with everyone you read. Even in an entertainment setting, you're fulfilling the role of a counselor and the words you say to people will be remembered verbatim for many years.

Consequently, it's important to put people at ease before starting to read their hands. You might like to start by offering your clients a cup of tea or coffee and chat casually with them for a few minutes before starting the reading.

Many people are terrified that you might see something tragic or unpleasant in their future. They may even think you'll tell them when they're going to die. Because of this, it's essential that you remain calm and relaxed, no matter what you may see in the person's hands. People will be observing your expressions and body language, and will immediately think you've seen something bad if you look horrified or startled. As a palm reader, you must not judge others. Everyone is different, and everyone is doing the best that he or she can. Be compassionate, try to bolster everyone's self-esteem, listen carefully, and give good impartial advice.

Some people will think you're the reincarnation of Nostradamus, and will want to consult you every five minutes. Conversely, you'll also come across your share of skeptics. Most people will fit somewhere between these two extremes. They'll be open-minded, curious, and interested in discovering what you can see in their hands, but aware they ultimately make their own destinies.

Remain modest about your skills. Reading palms is an opportunity to advise and help others—it is not an excuse for an ego trip. Enjoy your newfound popularity by all means, but keep your feet firmly on the ground.

Keep learning. Once you have mastered the material in this book, read as many other books on palmistry as possible. Visit a palmist and have your palms read. This is all part of your education in palmistry. However, once you know the basics, you'll learn most by reading as many hands as possible. The more you learn, the better your readings will become.

Your knowledge of palmistry will give you great satisfaction, and will enable you to help and advise many people. I wish you great success as a palmist.

NOTES

Introduction

1. Cheiro was one of the names used by William John Warner (1866–1936), the most famous palm reader of the later nineteenth and early twentieth centuries. He also used the name Count Louis Hamon.

2. Katharine St. Hill, *The Book of the Hand* (London: Rider and Company, 1927), 11.

3. Examples include: Blanka Schaumann and Milton Adler, *Dermatoglyphics in Medical Disorders* (New York: Springer Verlag New York Inc., 1976), Jamshed Mavalwala (ed.), *Dermatoglyphics: An International Perspective* (The Hague: Mouton Publishers, 1978), Amrita Bagga, *Dermatoglyphics of Schizophrenics* (New Delhi: Mittal Publications, 1989), R. S. Bali and Ramesh Chaube (eds.), Ralph M. Garruto et al., *Dermatoglyphics: Science in Transition* (New York: Wiley-Liss Publishing, 1991), *Application and Methodological Perspectives in Dermatoglyphics* (New Delhi:

Oscar Publications, 1994), Richard Unger, *Lifeprints: Deciphering Your Life Purpose from Your Fingerprints* (Berkeley, CA: Crossing Press, 2007), Ronelle Coburn, *Destiny at Your Fingertips* (Woodbury, MN: Llewellyn Publications, 2008).

Chapter Eight

1. William Benham, *The Laws of Scientific Hand Reading: A Practical Treatise on the Art Commonly Called Palmistry* (New York: Duell, Sloan and Pearce, revised ed. 1946), 562.

Chapter Nine

1. Norris M. Durham and Chris C. Plato, eds. *Trends in Dermatoglyphic Research* (Dordrecht, Netherlands: Kluwer Academic Publishers, 1990), 6.

GLOSSARY

AIR HAND—There are four main types of hands, named after the four elements of fire, earth, air and water. The air hand comprises a square-shaped palm and long fingers. People with air hands have good communication skills.

APOLLO FINGER—The Apollo finger is the third, or ring, finger. It is related to creativity and optimism.

ARCH—Arches are one of the three fingerprint patterns. They indicate that the person is reliable and dependable in the area indicated by the fingers it is found on.

DERMATOGLYPHICS—Dermatoglyphics is the term used to describe the skin ridge patterns found on the palm and fingers. Fingerprints are the best-known examples of these.

DESTINY LINE—The destiny line is one of the four major lines. It runs from the base of the palm toward the fingers, usually finishing under the Saturn (second) finger. Not everyone has a destiny line. When it is present, it gives the person a purpose or sense of direction in his or her life.

DOMINANT HAND—This is the person's right hand, if he or she is right-handed, or the left hand, if he or she is left-handed.

EARTH HAND—There are four main types of hands, named after the four elements of fire, earth, air and water. The earth hand comprises a square-shaped palm and short fingers. People with earth hands are practical and down-to-earth.

FIRE HAND—There are four main types of hands, named after the four elements of fire, earth, air and water. The fire hand comprises an oblong-shaped palm and short fingers. People with fire hands are enthusiastic and emotional.

GIRDLE OF VENUS—The Girdle of Venus is a line (or sometimes a series of small lines) running parallel to the heart line, between the heart line and the fingers. It shows that the person is emotionally sensitive and easily hurt.

HEAD LINE—The head line is one of the four major lines on the hand. It starts close to, or joining, the start of the life line and runs across the middle of the palm. It reveals the person's intelligence and way of thinking.

HEART LINE—The heart line is one of the four major lines on the palm. It is the major line that is closest to the fingers. It starts on the Mercury (little) finger side of the palm and runs across the middle of the palm. It reveals the person's emotional life.

HEPATICA—The hepatica is the health line. It starts close to the life line at the base of the hand and runs toward the Mercury (little) finger. It reveals the person's state of health. People without a hepatica line enjoy extremely good health.

ISLAND—An island is an enclosed oval shape in one of the main lines. It indicates a time when the person felt uncertainty and frustration. A series of islands creates a braiding or chainlike effect.

JUPITER FINGER—The Jupiter finger is the first, or index, finger. It relates to ambition, self-esteem, and the ego.

LIFE LINE—The life line is one of the four major lines on the palm. It encircles the thumb, and indicates the person's energy and vitality.

LOOP—Loops are one of the three fingerprint patterns. Approximately sixty-five percent of all fingerprints are loops, making this the most commonly found fingerprint pattern. Loops make the person easy to get along with.

There are also thirteen loops that can be found on the surface of the palm. These relate to different talents that the person who has one or more of them possesses.

MARRIAGE LINES—Marriage lines are fine lines on the Mercury (little) finger side of the palm, between the heart line and the base of the Mercury finger. They indicate important relationships.

MEDICAL STIGMATA—The medical stigmata consists of two or more short lines under the Mercury finger. It shows the person has a strong desire to help others.

MERCURY FINGER—The Mercury finger is the fourth, or little finger. It relates to communication, business ability, honesty, and shrewdness.

MOUNT OF APOLLO—The mount of Apollo is situated under the Apollo finger. If this mount is prominent on the hand, it indicates creativity, spontaneity, and a love of beauty.

MOUNT OF INNER MARS—The mount of inner mars is situated inside the life line, between the base of the thumb and the Jupiter finger. If this mount is prominent on the hand, it indicates drive, ambition, physical strength, and persistence.

MOUNT OF JUPITER—The mount of Jupiter is situated beneath the Jupiter finger. If this mount is prominent on the hand, it indicates confidence and leadership ability.

MOUNT OF LUNA—The mount of Luna lies at the base of the hand on the side of the Mercury (little) finger, directly opposite the thumb. If this mount is prominent on the hand, it indicates a quiet, intuitive, creative, and imaginative nature.

MOUNT OF MERCURY—The mount of Mercury is located under the Mercury (little) finger. If this mount is prominent on the hand, it indicates business ability, curiosity, and the ability to think quickly.

MOUNT OF NEPTUNE—The mount of Neptune is located at the base of the hand by the wrist, between the mounts of Luna and Venus. If this mount is prominent on the hand, it indicates the ability to think quickly and skill at public speaking.

MOUNT OF OUTER MARS—The mount of outer mars is situated between the heart and head lines on the Mercury (little) finger side of the palm. If this mount is prominent on the hand, it indicates courage, strength, and the ability to withstand the slings and arrows of life.

MOUNT OF VENUS—The mount of Venus is situated at the base of the thumb, and is the mound encircled by the life line. If this mount is prominent on the hand, it indicates love, passion, and energy.

MOUNTS—There are nine mounts on the palm, all named after different planets. They are usually slightly raised areas on the surface of the palm. They reveal the person's interests and talents.

MYSTIC CROSS—The mystic cross consists of two small lines that cross each other in the area between the heart and head lines. It shows that the person is interested in psychic matters.

PHALANGE—A phalange is one section of a finger or thumb. Each finger has three phalanges. The thumb appears to have only two, but the mound beneath the thumb that is encircled by the life line is considered to be the third phalange.

QUADRANGLE—The quadrangle is the area between the heart and head lines.

RASCETTES—The rascettes are lines that cross the wrist at the base of the hand forming what appear to be bracelets. Most people have three of these. Traditionally, palmists read these to determine health problems. However, they are ignored by most present-day palmists.

SATURN FINGER—The Saturn finger is the second finger. It is usually the longest finger on the hand. This finger relates to stability, wisdom, caution, and a serious approach to life.

SIMIAN CREASE—The simian crease occurs when the head and heart line form a single line that runs across the palm.

SISTER LINE—A sister line is a line that runs parallel to another line, giving it support. It is most frequently found inside the life line.

SQUARES—Squares are usually protective, especially when they surround breaks on the major lines.

TEACHER'S SQUARE—The teacher's square is a small square found under the Jupiter finger. It shows that the person has the ability to explain things clearly to others.

TRAVEL LINES—Travel lines are found on the Mercury (little) finger side of the palm in the area between the heart line and the wrist. They indicate a desire to travel.

TRI-RADII—The tri-radii (sing. tri-radius) are the small triangles formed by the skin ridge patterns when three ridge patterns meet. They indicate the highest point of the mounts below each finger. Tri-radii are also found on the top of the mount of Luna, and occasionally on the mount of Neptune.

VIA LASCIVA—The Via Lasciva is a well-marked minor line that starts some three-quarters of the way down the palm on the Mercury (little) finger side of the palm, and heads towards the thumb. It is usually a straight line, but can be slightly curved. It used to be associated with lasciviousness. Nowadays, it is interpreted to indicate that the person needs constant stimulation, and something to look forward to, in order to be happy.

WATER HAND—There are four main types of hands, named after the four elements of fire, earth, air and water. The water hand comprises an oblong palm and long fingers. People with water hands are sensitive and intuitive.

WHORL—Whorls are one of the three fingerprint patterns. They show that the person is slightly unorthodox in his or her approach to the concerns indicated by the finger or fingers the whorl is on.

WORRY LINES—Worry lines are the fine lines that radiate out from the base of the thumb towards the life line. This worry can affect the person's health if the lines cross the life line.

WRITER'S FORK—The writer's fork occurs when the end of the head line splits into two. This shows the person can come up with a good idea and make practical use of it.

SUGGESTED READING

Altman, Nathaniel. *The Palmistry Workbook*. Wellingborough, UK: The Aquarian Press, 1984.

———. *Sexual Palmistry*. Wellingborough, UK: The Aquarian Press, 1986. Republished as *Palmistry for Lovers*, 1993.

Asano, Hachiro. *Hands: The Complete Book of Palmistry*. Tokyo: Japan Publications, Inc., 1985.

Benham, William G. *The Laws of Scientific Handreading: A Practical Treatise on the Art Commonly Called Palmistry*. Revised ed. 1900, New York: Duell, Sloan and Pearce, 1946.

Brandon-Jones, David. *Practical Palmistry*. London: Rider and Company, 1981.

Brandon-Jones, David, and Veronica Bennett. *Your Palm—Barometer of Health*. London: Rider and Company, 1985.

Brenner, Elizabeth. *The Hand Book*. Berkeley CA: Celestial Arts, Inc., 1980.

Campbell, Edward D. *The Encyclopedia of Palmistry*. New York: Perigee Books, 1996.

Coburn, Ronelle. *Destiny at Your Fingertips*. Woodbury, MN: Llewellyn Publications, 2008.

Collins, Judith Hipskind. *The Hand from A to Z*. St. Paul, MN: Llewellyn Publications, 2005.

Cummins, Harold, and Charles Midlo. *Finger Prints, Palms and Soles: An Introduction to Dermatoglyphics*. Philadelphia: The Blakiston Company, 1943.

Dukes, Shifu Terence. *Chinese Hand Analysis*. York Beach, ME: Samuel Weiser, Inc., 1987.

Fincham, Johnny. *The Spellbinding Power of Palmistry: New Insights into an Ancient Art*. Sutton Mallet, UK: Green Magic, 2005.

Gale, Marion. *Read his Hands, Know his Heart*. Philadelphia: Running Press Books, 2005.

Garutto, Ralph M., Chris C. Plato, and Blanka A. Schaumann (eds.). *Dermatoglyphics: Science in Transition*. Wilmington, DE: Wiley-Liss, 1991.

Hipskind, Judith. *The New Palmistry*. St. Paul, MN: Llewellyn Publications, 1994.

Holtzman, Arnold. *The Illustrated Textbook of Psychodiagnostic Chirology in Analysis and Therapy*. Toronto: The Greenwood-Chase Press, 2004.

Hutchinson, Beryl. *Your Life in Your Hands*. London: Neville Spearman Limited, 1967.

Jaquin, Noel. *The Hand of Man*. London: Faber & Faber Limited, 1933.

———. *The Hand Speaks: Your Health, Your Sex, Your Life*. London: Lyndoe and Fisher Limited, 1942.

———. *Scientific Palmistry*. London: Cecil Palmer, 1925.

Lyon, Sheila, and Mark Sherman. *Palms Up!* New York: Berkley Books, 2005.

Masters, Anthony. *Mind Map*. London: Eyre Methuen Limited, 1980.

Nakagaichi, Mika. *Palmistry for the Global Village*. Tokyo: Tachibana Publishing, Inc., 1998.

Nishitani, Yasuto. *Palmistry Revolution*. Tokyo: Tachibana Shuppan, Inc., 1992.

Saint-Germain, Jon. *Runic Palmistry*. St. Paul, MN: Llewellyn Publications, 2001.

———. *A Lover's Guide to Palmistry: Finding Love in the Palm of Your Hand*. Woodbury, MN: Llewellyn Publications, 2008.

Schaumann, Blanka, and Milton Alter. *Dermatoglyphics in Medical Disorders*. New York: Springer-Verlag New York, Inc., 1976.

Sherson, R. *The Key to Your Hands*. Auckland, NZ: Mystical Books Company, 1973.

Spier, Julius. *The Hands of Children*. London: Kegan Paul, Trench, Trubner and Company, 1944.

Steinbach, Martin. *Medical Palmistry*. Secaucus, NJ: University Books, Inc., 1975.

Unger, Richard. *Lifeprints: Deciphering Your Life Purpose from your Fingerprints* Berkeley, CA: Crossing Press, 2007.

Webster, Richard. *Revealing Hands*. St. Paul, MN: Llewellyn Publications, 1994.

———. *Palm Reading for Beginners*. St. Paul, MN: Llewellyn Publications, 2000.

Wolff, Charlotte. *The Hand in Psychological Diagnosis*. New York: Philosophical Library, 1952.

INDEX

A

air hand, 15–16, 18, 91–92, 164, 180
Alexander the Great, 4
Angle of Pitch, 48
Angle of Practicality, 2, 47–48, 166–167, 186
Angle of Time, 47
apex
    of Apollo, 138
    of Jupiter, 136
    of Mercury, 138
    of Saturn, 137
Apollo finger, 34–35, 37–41, 93, 131, 133–135, 137–139, 169
Arch
    tented, 134–135
Aristotle, 4
D'Arpentigny, Captain Casimir Stanislaus, 5–6, 19–21
Avicenna, 4

B

Benham, William G., 6–7, 22, 113
Bonaparte, Napoleon, 43
bracelets, 126
breaks, 50, 59, 66, 73, 79–80, 90, 92, 112, 114–115, 147–148, 156

C

Carus, Carl, 22
chains, 50, 58, 66, 73–74, 152, 156, 159–160
Cheiro, 3
cheirognomy, 9
Children lines, 121–122, 156–157
chirology, 50
circles, 26, 132, 151
coarse hands, 85–86

color
　nail, 30
　palm, 87
compatibility, 101, 157–160,
　　162
cone, 20, 29, 48
conic hands, 20
consistency, 84
crosses, 54, 59–60, 80, 92, 112,
　　125–126, 147–149
Cummins, Dr Harold, 129

D
dermatoglyphics, 7, 127, 129,
　　145, 173, 180
Desbarolles, Adrien Adolphe,
　　6
destiny line, 51–53, 75–81, 92,
　　94, 114, 118, 124, 144,
　　148–149, 152, 170–171,
　　179, 182, 186
dots, 151
Down's syndrome, 67, 143
dropped little finger, 29, 33,
　　93

E
earth hand, 15–17, 86, 90, 164,
　　173
elements, 13, 17, 22–23
elementary hand, 20

F
fate line, 75
fingernail, 30–31, 34, 86–87
Finger of Sacrifice, 39
fingerprints, 130–132, 183
fingers
　length, 6, 11, 27, 33–34,
　　37–38, 171
　short, 2, 11–15, 20, 25, 32–
　　33, 35–36, 87, 164–165
　long, 2, 12–13, 16–17, 20,
　　32–33, 35–38, 164–165,
　　170–171, 180, 183
　medium-length, 11–12, 21,
　　44, 46, 90
finger setting, 28–29, 33, 183,
　　186
fingertips, 20–21, 26, 29, 132,
　　167
fire hand, 14–16, 18, 165
flexibility, 11, 49, 88, 91, 130,
　　160, 175–176, 179
Flower Line, 50
four elements, the, 13, 22

G
Galton, Sir Francis, 130
Girdle of Venus, 52, 59, 156–
　　157, 179, 182
Grilles, 150–151
guardian angel line, 70
Gypsies, 5, 126

H

Hadrian, Emperor, 4
hair, 86
hand prints
    how to take, 173
Hartlieb, Johannes, 5
head line
    imaginative, 63
    practical, 63–64
Health line, 112–113, 149, 184
Heart line, 51–60, 70, 80–81,
        91, 93, 107, 112, 116,
        120, 152, 156–161, 180,
        182, 188
Hepatica, see health line
Herschel, Sir William, 129
Humanitarian loop, 140, 144

I

islands, 58–59, 73–74, 112,
        114, 152, 156

J

John of Salisbury, 4
Jung, Carl, 7
Jupiter finger, 35–41, 44, 46,
        50, 55, 57, 93, 130, 132–
        137, 141, 159, 166, 170–
        171, 188
Juvenal, 4

K

Kennedy-Galton Centre, 7
knotty fingers, 26
knotty hand, 20–21

L

leaning fingers, 39
Lévi, Eliphas, 6
Life line, 51–53, 60–62, 66–67,
        69–71, 73–75, 77–78, 90,
        92–94, 97, 100–101, 106,
        112, 115, 120, 125, 141,
        147–148, 151, 182, 188
Line of Apollo, 114
Line of intuition, 117–118,
    186
Line of Mars, 70, 115
Line of Mercury, 112
liver line, see health line
loop of
    common sense, 140–141,
        188
    courage, 140–142
    ego, 139–141
    good intent, 141
    humor, 139–140, 156–157
    inspiration, 140, 143
    memory, 140, 144–145
    music, 140, 142, 144, 170
    recall, 140, 145
    response, 140, 142, 170
    stringed music, 140, 144,
        170

loops
    fingerprint type, 131, 139,
        141, 184
loyalty line, 120

M
marriage, 120–121, 149
Mars line, 120
medical stigmata, 123, 166,
    168
mental heart line, 54–55, 158–
    159
Mercury finger, 32–33, 39–41,
        93, 105, 121, 131, 133–
        135, 138, 161, 166, 169–
        171, 180, 186, 188
Mercury line, 112, 171, 186
money
    earned, 124
    inherited, 124
    triangle, 125
    won, 124
mount of Apollo, 99, 104–105,
        139, 151, 169
mount of Jupiter, 62, 99, 102–
        103, 136, 144, 149–151
mount of Luna, 78, 97, 99,
        108–109, 119, 136, 143–
        144, 151, 156, 168–169,
        186
mount of Mars
    inner, 99, 106–107, 120,
        141, 168

outer, 99, 106–107, 120,
    141, 168
mount of Mercury, 99, 105–
    106, 112, 151
mount of Neptune, 97, 109,
    136, 143
mount of Saturn, 99, 103–
    104, 137, 151
mount of Venus, 44, 47, 50,
    60, 69–70, 74, 97, 99–
    101, 106, 115, 142, 144,
    148–150, 156–157, 160,
    168–169
Murderer's Thumb, 49
mystic cross, 125–126

P
phalanges
    tip, 25, 30, 33–34, 36–38,
        44–45
    middle, 26, 33, 38, 167
    base, 26, 34–35, 37, 39, 44,
        46, 49
philosophic hands, 21
physical heart line, 55, 91, 93,
    158–159
plain of Mars, 107–108
Pliny, 4
pointed hand, 21
protective square, 112, 115
psychic hand, 21

Q

quadrangle, 80, 94, 125, 145, 149, 184

R

rajah loop, 140–141
rascettes, 126
Refined hands, 85–86
relationship lines, 52, 120–121, 156–157, 161, 184
restlessness lines, see travel lines
ring of Saturn, 118–119
Ring of Solomon, 117
rings, 41

S

Santander Caves, 3
Saturn finger, 36–38, 40–41, 56–58, 74, 94, 105, 130, 133–138, 141, 159
Sigismund, 4
simian crease, 67–69
sister line, 52, 70, 72, 90, 115, 179, 182
skin texture, 85–86
smooth joints, 26, 37
spatulate
    fingertips, 29
    hands, see spatulate hands
spatulate hands, 20
Spier, Julius, 7

spots
    on the nails, 31
square hands, 21
squares, 73, 147
stars, 147, 150,
St. Hill, Katharine, 3
strain lines, 32
stress lines, 32
sun line, 113–115

T

teacher's square, 122–123, 166, 184, 188
tented arch, see arch, tented
texture, 6, 85–86, 88, 176
thumb
    angle of, 46–47, 92
length of
    setting of, 46, 91–92
    tip, 44, 48
timing
    events, 112
    in angles, 47–48
travel lines, 116–117, 184
Triangles, 124–125, 136, 147, 149, 184, 188
Tri-radii, 136–139, 145

U

ulnar loop, 131, 140, 143

V

Via Lasciva, 119

W

waisted phalange, 46, 48, 90

water hand, 15–17, 19, 59, 86, 165, 173

Wheat Line, 50

whorls, 130–133, 183

willpower
and logic, 44, 53, 91–92, 183

worry lines, 52, 70, 72–73, 90, 92, 94, 120, 182

writer's fork, 65, 92–94, 169, 180, 182

Aura Reading for Beginners
Develop Your Psychic Awareness for Health & Success
Richard Webster

When you lose your temper, don't be surprised if a dirty red haze suddenly appears around you. If you do something magnanimous, your aura will expand. Now you can learn to see the energy that emanates off yourself and other people through the proven methods taught by Richard Webster in his psychic training classes.

Learn to feel the aura, see the colors in it, and interpret what those colors mean. Explore the chakra system, and how to restore balance to chakras that are over- or under-stimulated. Then you can begin to imprint your desires into your aura to attract what you want in your life.

978-1-56718-798-4
208 pp., 5³⁄₁₆ x 8 $13.99

CHANGE AT HAND
Balancing Your Energy Through Palmistry, Chakras & Mudras
SANDRA KYNES

The power of energetic balance is in your hands. *Change at Hand* uniquely combines the wisdom of palmistry with the power of the elements to help you manifest change in your life.

Popular author Sandra Kynes teaches you how to read your palms and circulate energy with your hands to discover and actualize your true potentials. Practice mudras (specific hand positions and gestures) to activate and direct life force energy for healing and enlightenment. Use crystals to open your hand chakras. Get a better understanding of your personality by determining your elemental archetype and interpreting your palm's shape, your heart and life line, your finger lengths, and more.

978 0 7387 1570 4
240 pp., 7½ x 9⅛ $17.95

TO ORDER, CALL 1-877-NEW-WRLD
Prices subject to change without notice
Order at Llewellyn.com 24 hours a day, 7 days a week!

NUMEROLOGY FOR BEGINNERS
Easy Guide to Love, Money, Destiny
GERIE BAUER

Every letter and number in civilization has a particular power, or vibration. For centuries, people have read these vibrations through the practice of numerology. References in the Bible even describe Jesus using numerology to change the names of his disciples. *Numerology for Beginners* is a quick ready-to-use reference that lets you find your personal vibrations based on the numbers associated with your birthdate and name.

Within minutes, you will be able to assess the vibrations surrounding a specific year, month, and day—even a specific person. Detect whether you're in a business cycle or a social cycle, and whether a certain someone or occupation would be compatible with you. Plus, learn to detect someone's personality within seconds of learning his/her first name!

978-1-56718-057-2
336 pp., 5³⁄₁₆ x 8 $13.95

INSTANT PALM READER
A Road Map to Life
LINDA DOMIN

Etched upon your palm is an aerial view of all the scenes you will travel in the course of your lifetime. Your characteristics, skills, and abilities are imprinted in your mind and transferred as images on to your hand. Now, with this simple, flip-through pictorial guide, you can assemble your own personal palm reading, like a professional, almost instantly.

The *Instant Palm Reader* shows you how your hands contain the picture of the real you—physically, emotionally, and mentally. More than 500 easy-to-read diagrams will provide you with candid, uplifting revelations about yourself: personality, childhood, career, finances, family, love life, talents, and destiny.

With the sensitive information artfully contained within each interpretation, you will also be able to uncover your hidden feelings and unconscious needs as you learn the secrets of this 3,000-year-old science.

978-1-56718-232-3
256 pp., 7 x 10 $16.95

A Practical Guide to the Runes
Their Uses in Divination and Magick
Lisa Peschel

At last the world has a beginner's book on the Nordic runes that is written in straightforward and clear language. Each of the twenty-five runes is elucidated through no-nonsense descriptions and clean graphics. A rune's altered meaning in relation to other runes and its reversed position is also included. The construction of runes and accessories covers such factors as the type of wood to be used, the size of the runes, and the coloration, carving, and charging of the runes.

With this book the runes can be used in magick to effect desired results. Talismans carved with runescripts or bindrunes allow you to carry your magick in a tangible form, providing foci for your will. Four rune layouts complete with diagrams are presented with examples of specific questions to ask when consulting the runes. Rather than simple fortunetelling devices, the runes are oracular, empowered with the forces of Nature. They present information for you to make choices in your life.

978-0-87542-593-1

192 pp., 4³⁄₁₆ x 6⅞ $6.99

FENG SHUI FOR BEGINNERS
Successful Living by Design
RICHARD WEBSTER

Not advancing fast enough in your career? Maybe your desk is located in a "negative position." Wish you had a more peaceful family life? Hang a mirror in your dining room and watch what happens. Is money flowing out of your life rather than into it? You may want to look to the construction of your staircase!

For thousands of years, the ancient art of feng shui has helped people harness universal forces and lead lives rich in good health, wealth, and happiness. The basic techniques in *Feng Shui for Beginners* are very simple, and you can put them into place immediately in your home and work environments. Gain peace of mind, a quiet confidence, and turn adversity to your advantage with feng shui remedies.

978-1-56718-803-5
288 pp., 5¼ x 8 $13.95

PRACTICAL GUIDE TO PSYCHIC POWERS
Awaken Your Sixth Sense
DENNING & PHILLIPS

Because you are missing out on so much without them! Who has not dreamed of possessing powers to move objects without physically touching them, to see at a distance or into the future, to know another's thoughts, to read the past of an object or person, or to find water or mineral wealth by dowsing?

This book is a complete course—teaching you step-by-step how to develop the powers that actually have been yours since birth. Psychic powers are a natural part of your mind; by expanding your mind in this way, you will gain health and vitality, emotional strength, greater success in your daily pursuits, and a new understanding of your inner self.

You'll learn to play with these new skills, working with groups of friends to accomplish things you never would have believed possible. The text shows you how to make the equipment, do the exercises—many of them at any time, anywhere—and how to use your abilities to change your life and the lives of those close to you.

978-0-87542-191-9
288 pp., 5³⁄₁₆ x 8 $12.95

JEWELRY & GEMS FOR SELF-DISCOVERY
Choosing Gemstones That Delight the Eye and Strengthen the Soul
SHAKTI CAROLA NAVRAN

Have you ever fallen in love with a ring or necklace? Perhaps there's a reason! Gems and crystals have metaphysical and healing qualities that can support you physically, emotionally, and spiritually. This innovative guide will help you choose a piece of jewelry ideal for your unique life path.

Diamonds enhance your creativity. Rubies teach us about love. Opals fuel intuition and offer healing. Which stones are right for you? Shakti Carola Navran offers a thorough introduction to astrology to help you identify the challenges and spiritual needs evident in your birth chart. A detailed list of sixty-four gems and crystals—with full-color photos of polished stones and finished jewelry—makes it easy to find the minerals that can balance these conflicting energies. You'll learn how to "program" your stone with joy, peace of mind, self-confidence, or any other quality. There's also helpful information for choosing the form (ring, earrings, or necklace), selecting the metal setting, and incorporating symbols into your unique piece of jewelry.

978-0-7387-1443-1
216 pp., 6 x 9 $16.95

You Are Psychic
The Art of Clairvoyant Reading & Healing
Debra Lynne Katz

Learn to see inside yourself and others. Clairvoyance is the ability to see information—in the form of visions and images—through nonphysical means. According to Debra Lynne Katz, anyone who can visualize a simple shape, such as a circle, has clairvoyant ability.

In *You Are Psychic*, Katz shares her own experiences and methods for developing these clairvoyant skills. Her techniques and psychic tools are easy to follow and have been proven to work by long-time practitioners. Psychic readings, healing methods, vision interpretation, and spiritual counseling are all covered in this practical guide to clairvoyance.

978-0-7387-0592-7
336 pp., 6 x 9 $16.95